# Questions
# young people ask
## answers that work
**VOLUME 2**

this book is the property of

D1009172

Publishers
WATCHTOWER BIBLE AND TRACT SOCIETY OF NEW YORK, INC.
Brooklyn, New York, U.S.A.
2008 Printing

This publication is provided as part of a worldwide Bible educational work
supported by voluntary donations

Unless otherwise indicated, Scripture quotations are from the modern-language
*New World Translation of the Holy Scriptures—With References*

The names of some of the youths in this book have been changed

Photo Credits: Page 165: Woman with firewood: Godo-Foto;
European city: © 2003 BiblePlaces.com

*Questions Young People Ask—Answers That Work*, Volume 2          English (*yp2*-E)
Made in the United States of America

# ■ A Note to Parents

To young people, going through adolescence can be like walking a tightrope. Each step may seem uncertain —even frightening. As a parent, you may sometimes wish you could spare your young ones this particular "walk." You can't, of course, but you *can* be their balancing pole. You are in a unique position to help your children stay on course and emerge from their adolescence as responsible adults.

Easier said than done? Certainly. It may seem like only yesterday that your son was an energetic toddler who wouldn't keep quiet; now he's a withdrawn teen who won't talk to you. Not long ago your little girl wanted to go everywhere with you; now she seems mortified at the very idea of being seen in public with her parents!

Yet, you need not feel inadequate when facing these changes. You have access to a source of wisdom that can provide solid guidance for you and your child. That source of wisdom is God's Word, the Bible.

*Questions Young People Ask—Answers That Work,* Volume 2, is designed to provide your child with solid reasoning from the Scriptures. A look at Contents on pages 4 and 5 will give you an idea of the variety of topics covered. But this publication will do more than present the facts. Consider the following:

(1) The book is interactive. In many places your child will be prompted to write down his or her response to various questions and statements. For example, the "Peer-Pressure Planner" on pages 132 and 133 will help your child think about specific challenges he or she faces and ways to respond to them. In addition, each of this

book's nine sections concludes with a page entitled "My Journal," in which your child can write personal thoughts and feelings on the material contained in that section.

(2) The book promotes communication. For example, pages 63 and 64 contain the box "How Can I Talk to Dad or Mom About Sex?" Also, at the end of each chapter, there is a box entitled "What Do You Think?" More than a review, this box can be used as an outline for family discussion. In addition, each chapter contains an "Action Plan!" the last segment of which asks the young person to complete this sentence: "What I would like to ask my parent(s) about this subject is . . ." This will encourage youths to look to their parents for balanced advice as they walk the tightrope of adolescence.

A word of caution: To encourage your adolescents to write in their book with candor, allow them a measure of privacy. Later they may well open up to you on the issues they have written about.

Obtain your own copy of this book, and become thoroughly familiar with it. As you read, try to recall all the drama, confusion, and anxiety that were part of your own adolescence. When appropriate, share your experiences with your son or daughter. That will encourage your young ones to confide in you. When they talk, listen! If efforts to communicate seem futile, do not give up. No matter how much they may indicate otherwise, children tend to value the advice of their parents more than that of their peers.

It is our pleasure to provide both you and your children with this Bible-based tool, and it is our prayer that it will prove to be a blessing to your family.

**The Publishers**

3

# contents

### for girls

You can't help but think about the gorgeous new boy in class. 'He doesn't even know I exist,' you tell yourself, 'so, what harm is there in daydreaming?' Besides, it's not just you. This boy is every girl's dream. You know that because you hear the other girls talking about him all the time.

Suddenly he's looking in your direction. He catches you off guard with his disarming smile. You smile back. He approaches.

"Hi," he says shyly.

"Hey," you say back.

"I'm Brett."

### for boys

Two of your schoolmates are approaching. You feel a knot in your stomach because twice already this week they've tried to get you to smoke. This will be their third attempt.

The first boy speaks: "All alone again? Let me introduce you to a friend." He underscores the word "friend" with a wink as he takes something out of his pocket and extends his hand toward you.

You see something between the boy's thumb and forefinger that resembles a cigarette. You know exactly what it is, and the knot in your stomach gets even tighter.

:: *"You're new here,"* you blurt out.

*"My family just moved in a few weeks ago."*

*You still can't believe that Brett is actually talking to you!*

*"Look,"* Brett continues, *"I'm having a party at my house after school today. Want to come?"*

*Then he leans forward and winks.*

*"Let me warn you,"* he says. *"My parents aren't home, and the liquor cabinet isn't locked. What do you say?"*

*Brett is waiting for your reply. Any other girl in your school would say yes immediately!*

*What will you say?*

:: *"Sorry,"* you say. *"I've already told you I don't . . ."*

*The second boy interrupts:* *"It's that religion of yours, isn't it? You can't have any fun!"*

*"Or are you just chicken?"* the first boy taunts.

*"No, I'm not chicken!"* you summon the courage to say.

*Then the second boy places his arm around your shoulder.* *"Just take it,"* he says softly.

*The first boy moves the white object closer to your face and adds in a hushed voice:* *"We won't tell anyone. No one will ever know."*

*What will you do?*

SIMILAR scenes are played out every day in virtually every part of the globe. The fact is, though, that some young people are better prepared than others to handle such situations. In the pressure of the moment, a boy being tempted to smoke might think: 'I don't want to give in, but I can't take any more pressure. Why can't I show my schoolmates that I can be "normal"?' Or a girl who's asked out on a date might say to herself: 'He's clean-cut. For once—just this once—why can't I say *yes?*'

On the other hand, many youths have been trained to stand up confidently for what they believe. As a result —strange as it may seem—they feel *less* pressure to do wrong. Would you like to be that kind of youth? The good news is that you *can* be! How?

The Bible can help you to face the challenges of youth with confidence. It contains the best advice to be found because it's the inspired Word of God. (2 Timothy 3:16, 17) What types of issues can the Bible help you with? Look at the list below, and put a ✔ next to the topics that particularly appeal to *you.*

- ❑ Relating to the opposite sex
- ❑ Coming to terms with my body
- ❑ Making friends
- ❑ Surviving school
- ❑ Managing my money
- ❑ Dealing with my parents
- ❑ Controlling my feelings
- ❑ Exploring my recreation options
- ❑ Improving my spirituality

As you will note on pages 4 and 5, the topics list-ed above correspond to the nine sections of this book. Which ones did you mark? You might want to consult those sections first. Bible principles can help you in each of these areas of life. The book you're now reading will show you how.*

This book will also provide you with opportunities to express your thoughts. For example, near the end of each chapter, you'll find a box entitled "Action Plan!" There you will be asked to record your thoughts on how you can apply what you've read. Worksheets —such as the "Peer-Pressure Planner" on pages 132 and 133—will help you to think through the challenges you face and to create practical solutions. In addition, each section of this book concludes with a page entitled "My Journal," which will allow you to write about how a particular aspect of the material applies to your life. You will also find at points throughout the book nine pages entitled "Role Model." In these, various Bible characters are highlighted as being worthy of imitation.

The Bible urges you: "Acquire wisdom, acquire understanding." (Proverbs 4:5) The words "wisdom" and "understanding" imply more than simply *knowing* right from wrong. You need to see the big picture. For example, knowing the consequences of a wrong course as well as the rewards for doing what is right will help you to face up to peer pressure with confidence and courage.

Be assured of this: Your problems—overwhelming as they may seem—are not unique. Others have faced and successfully dealt with challenges like yours. You can too! Make good use of *Questions Young People Ask—Answers That Work*, Volume 2. It will convince you that the Bible contains the *best* advice to be found anywhere!

* Much of this book has been compiled from selected articles that have appeared in the series "Young People Ask," which is a regular feature in *Awake!* magazine, published by Jehovah's Witnesses.

# this book contains . . .

**key scriptures that highlight main points**

### TIP

practical suggestions that will help you succeed

### DID YOU KNOW . . .

facts that will stimulate your thinking

## action plan!

✎ opportunities to express how you will put the material to use

### WHAT DO YOU THINK?

● questions that will help you reason on what you've read

## in addition . . .

*my journal*

each section of this book ends with a journal page that will allow you to put your thoughts into words

### ROLE MODEL

selected Bible characters are featured as worthy of imitation

# THE OPPOSITE SEX 1

**You see a boy and girl holding hands as they stroll down the school corridor between classes. How do you feel?**

❑ Don't care
❑ Slightly jealous
❑ Completely envious

**You're at the movies with friends when you realize that everyone is paired off—except you! How do you feel?**

❑ No problem
❑ Somewhat awkward
❑ Very jealous

**Your best friend has recently begun showing interest in a member of the opposite sex and is now dating. How do you feel?**

❑ Happy
❑ Slightly envious
❑ Resentful

Boy and girl, girl and boy. They're everywhere you look—in school, on the street, at the mall. Each time you see them, you feel a powerful urge to be part of that unit called a couple. But are you ready to date? If you *are,* how can you find someone who's right for you? If you do find someone, how can you keep the relationship clean while dating? **Chapters 1-5** will help you answer those questions.

# Am I ready to date?

*"There's a ton of pressure all around me to date. There's also a ton of cute guys."—Whitney.*

*"Some girls come on strong, and I want to say yes. But if I ask my parents, I know what their answer will be."—Phillip.*

THE urge to be with someone special—and to be with someone who thinks *you* are special—can be incredibly strong, even at a very young age. "I started to feel the pressure to date when I was 11," recalls Jenifer. Brittany says: "At school you feel like you're only half a person if you're not dating someone—anyone!"

What about you? Are *you* ready to date? To answer that, we first need to address a more basic question:

## What Is "Dating"?

Mark your response to the following questions:

*You regularly go out with a certain member of the opposite sex. Are you dating?*
□ Yes
□ No

*You and a member of the opposite sex are attracted to each other. Several times a day, you text-message or talk to this person on the phone. Are you dating?*
□ Yes
□ No

*Every time you get together with your friends, you pair off with the same person of the opposite sex. Are you dating?*
□ Yes
□ No

You most likely had no problem answering the first question. But you may have paused before responding to the second and the third. What exactly *is* dating? Really, dating is any social activity in which your romantic interest is focused on one particular person and that person's interest is focused on you. So the answer to all three questions listed above is *yes*. Whether on the phone or face-to-face, in the open or in secret, if you and a friend of the opposite sex have a special romantic understanding and communicate regularly, it's dating. Are you ready to go down that road? A consideration of three questions will help you find out.

## Why Do You Want to Date?

In many cultures dating is regarded as a legitimate way for two people to become better acquainted. But dating should have an honorable purpose—to help a young man and woman determine if they want to get married to each other.

Granted, some of your peers might take a casual view of dating. Perhaps they simply enjoy being with a special friend of the opposite sex, without any intention of

*If you date with no intention of marriage, you are acting like a child who plays with a new toy and then discards it*

marriage. Some might even view such a friend as little more than a trophy or an accessory to be seen with in public to boost their own self-esteem. Often, though, such shallow relationships are short-lived. "Many young ones who date break up with each other a week or two later," says a girl named Heather. "They come to view relationships as transitory—which in a sense prepares them for divorce rather than for marriage."

Clearly, when you date someone, you're affecting that person's feelings. So be sure your intentions are honorable. Think: Would you like someone to play with your feelings as if they were some child's toy—to be picked up for a moment and then quickly abandoned? A youth named Chelsea says: "Part of me wants to say that dating should be just for fun, but it's no fun when one person is taking it seriously and the other isn't."

## You're *How* Old?

At what age do you think it's appropriate for a youth to start dating? ✎............

Now ask one or both of your parents the same question, and fill in their answer. ............

Chances are, the first number you wrote down is lower than the second. Or maybe not! You might be among the many youths who are wisely putting off dating until

READ MORE ABOUT THIS TOPIC IN VOLUME 1, CHAPTERS 29 AND 30

they're old enough to know themselves better. That's what Danielle, 17, decided to do. She says: "Thinking back to two years ago, what I would have looked for in a potential mate was so different from what I would look for now. Basically, even at this point I don't trust myself to make such a decision. When I feel that my personality has been stable for a couple of years, then I'll think about dating."

There's another reason why waiting is wise. The Bible uses the phrase "the bloom of youth" to describe the period of life when sexual feelings and romantic emotions first become strong. (1 Corinthians 7:36) To maintain close association with one particular member of the opposite sex while you're still in this phase can fan the flames of desire and lead to wrong conduct. True, that might mean little to your peers. Many of them are all too eager to experiment with sex. But you can rise above that kind of thinking! (Romans 12:2) After all, the Bible urges you to "flee from sexual immorality." (1 Corinthians 6:18, *New International Version*) By waiting until you're past the bloom of youth, you can "ward off calamity."—Ecclesiastes 11:10.

## Are You Ready to Get Married?

To help you answer the above question, take a good look at yourself. Consider the following:

> *I think you should date someone when that person really means something to you and you feel your future together has potential. You care about a person, not just the idea of dating.* — *Amber*

**Relationships.** How do you treat your parents and siblings? Do you often lose your self-control with them, perhaps using harsh or sarcastic language to make a point? What would *they* say about you in that regard? How you deal with family members indicates how you will treat a mate.—Read Ephesians 4:31.

**Demeanor.** Are you positive or pessimistic? Are you reasonable, or do you always insist on doing things a certain way—*your* way? Can you keep calm when under pressure? Are you patient? Cultivating the fruitage of God's spirit now will help you prepare for being a husband or a wife later.—Read Galatians 5:22, 23.

**Finances.** How well do you handle money? Are you often in debt? Can you hold down a job? If not, why not? Is it because of the job? the employer? Or is it because of some habit or trait that you need to work on? If you have trouble handling your own finances, how will you manage those of a family?—Read 1 Timothy 5:8.

**Spirituality.** If you're one of Jehovah's Witnesses, what are your spiritual attributes? Do you take the initiative to read God's Word, to engage in the ministry, and to participate at Christian meetings?

✔ **TIP**

To prepare for dating and marriage, read 2 Peter 1: 5-7 and pick one quality you need to work on. In a month's time, see how much you have learned about—and improved in—that quality.

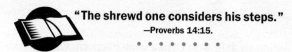

**"The shrewd one considers his steps."**
—Proverbs 14:15.

• • • • • • • •

The person you marry deserves nothing less than a spiritually strong partner.—Read Ecclesiastes 4:9, 10.

**What You *Can* Do**

Being pressured to date before you're ready would be like being forced to take a final exam for a course that you've barely started. Obviously, that wouldn't be fair! You need time to study your subject so you can become familiar with the kind of problems you'll face in the test.

It's similar with dating. As we've seen, dating is no trivial matter. So before you're ready to focus on one particular person, you need to take time to study a very important "subject"—how to build friendships. Later, when you meet the right person, you'll be in a better position to build a solid

### action plan!

*To prepare for marriage, I need to work on the following qualities:*

.................................................................

.................................................................

*I can work on these qualities by*

.................................................................

.................................................................

*What I would like to ask my parent(s) about this subject is*

.................................................................

.................................................................

relationship. After all, a good marriage is the union of two good friends.

Waiting to date won't stifle your freedom. On the contrary, it will give you *more* freedom to 'rejoice in your youth.' (Ecclesiastes 11:9) And you'll have time to prepare yourself by developing your personality and, most important, your spirituality.—Lamentations 3:27.

In the meantime, you *can* enjoy the company of the opposite sex. What's the best way to do so? Associate together in properly supervised mixed groups. A girl named Tammy says: "I think it's more fun that way. It's better to have a lot of friends." Monica agrees. "The group idea is a really good idea," she says, "because you get to see people with different personalities."

In contrast, if you focus on one person too soon, you set yourself up for heartache. So take your time. Use this period of your life to learn how to cultivate and maintain friendships. Later, if you choose to date, you'll have a better idea of who you are and what you need in a lifelong partner.

**IN OUR NEXT CHAPTER** *Tempted to date behind your parents' backs? There are more pitfalls to the practice than you may realize.*

**WHAT DO YOU THINK?**

- **In what appropriate settings can you mix with members of the opposite sex?**

- **How would you reason with a sibling who is too young to date but wants to do so?**

- **If you date but have no intention of marriage, how might that affect the other person's feelings?**

# 2

# Secret dating —what's the harm?

*Jessica was caught in a dilemma. It all started when a classmate named Jeremy began showing interest in her. "He was very cute," she says, "and my friends said he was the most decent boy I'd ever meet. Several girls had tried to start a relationship with him, but he wasn't interested in them. He liked only me."*

*Before long, Jeremy asked Jessica out. Jessica explained that as one of Jehovah's Witnesses, she wouldn't be allowed to date someone who wasn't of her faith. "But then Jeremy had an idea," she says. "He asked, 'Why can't we just date behind your parents' backs?'"*

IF SOMEONE *you* were attracted to made such a suggestion, how would you respond? You might be surprised to learn that Jessica agreed to Jeremy's plan. "I was convinced that if I dated him, I could make him learn to love Jehovah," she says. How did things turn out? We'll find out later. First, let's see how some get caught in the snare of secret dating.

## Why They Do It

Why do some date *secretly?* A young man named David puts it concisely, "They know their parents would not approve, so they don't tell them." Jane points out another possibility. "Secret dating is a rebellion thing," she says. "If you feel that you're not being treated like the young adult you think you are, you decide that you're going to do what you want and just not tell your parents."

Can you think of any other reasons why some might be tempted to date secretly? If so, list them below.

✎ ...............................................................................

...............................................................................

Of course, you realize that the Bible commands you to obey your parents. (Ephesians 6:1) And if your parents object to your dating, they must have a good reason. Still, don't be surprised if you find yourself thinking:

● *I feel left out because everyone is dating except me.*

● *I'm attracted to someone who doesn't share my faith.*

● *I would like to go out with a fellow Christian, even though I'm too young to marry.*

You probably know what your parents would say about the above statements. And deep down, you know that your parents are right. At the same time, you may feel like a girl named Manami, who says:

"The pressure to date is so strong that I sometimes doubt my stand. For kids today it's unthinkable *not* to be dating. Besides, it's no fun being by myself!" Some in that situation have begun to date, hiding the matter from their parents. How?

## "We Were Told to Keep It a Secret"

The very term "secret dating" suggests a measure of deception, and that's just what it takes to make it work. Some keep their dating secret by communicating primarily over the phone or the Internet. In public, they're just friends, but their e-mails, phone calls, and text messages tell a completely different story.

Another sly tactic is to arrange for a group activity, only to pair off later. James says: "Once, a group of us were invited to meet at a location, only to discover that the whole thing had been set up so that two in the group could be together. We were told to keep it a secret."

Frequently, as James points out, secret dating is carried on with the cooperation of friends. "Often, at least one friend knows about the situation but chooses not to say anything because of a 'don't-tell' mentality," says Carol. At times, blatant dishonesty is involved. "Many keep their dating secret by lying to their parents about where they go," says 17-year-old Beth. Misaki, 19, did just that. "I had to make up stories carefully," she says. "I was cautious not to tell any lies other than those related to my dating so that I would not lose my parents' trust."

**DID YOU KNOW...**

Lasting relationships are built on trust. Dating secretly betrays the trust of your parents and undermines the very foundation of your relationship with the one you're dating.

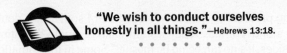

**"We wish to conduct ourselves honestly in all things."**—Hebrews 13:18.

· · · · · · · · ·

## The Pitfalls of Secret Dating

If you're tempted to date secretly—or if you're already doing so—you need to ask yourself the following two questions:

*Where will my course lead?* Do you intend to marry the person reasonably soon? "Dating without the intention of marriage is like advertising something you're not selling," says 20-year-old Evan. What can result? Proverbs 13:12 says: "Expectation postponed is making the heart sick." Do you really want to make someone you care about sick at heart? Another caution: Dating secretly will rob you of the loving interest of your parents and other concerned adults. Because of this, you're more likely to fall into the trap of sexual immorality.—Galatians 6:7.

*How does Jehovah God feel about what I'm doing?* The Bible says: "All things are naked and openly exposed to the eyes of him with whom we have an accounting." (Hebrews 4:13) So if you're covering up your own dating—or that of a friend—Jehovah already knows about it. And if deception is involved, you have good reason to be concerned. Jehovah God feels strongly about lying. Indeed, "a false tongue" is listed prominently in the Bible among the things that he detests!—Proverbs 6:16-19.

## Ending the Secrecy

Certainly, you would do well to talk to your parents or a mature Christian adult about any secret relationship that you may be involved in. And if a friend of yours is dating secretly, don't share in his or her course by helping to cover

*Covering up for a friend who is secretly dating is like covering up for a diabetic who is secretly gorging on sweets*

it up. (1 Timothy 5:22) After all, how would you feel if the relationship had harmful consequences? Wouldn't you be at least partly responsible?

To illustrate: Suppose a friend is diabetic and is secretly filling up on sweets. What if you found out about it, but your friend begged you not to tell anyone? What would be your greatest concern—covering up for your friend or taking action that could possibly save his or her life?

You face a similar situation if you know that an acquaintance is dating secretly. Don't worry about permanently ruining your friendship. In time, a true friend will realize that you were acting in his or her best interests.—Psalm 141:5.

**Secrecy or Privacy?**

Of course, not all secrecy surrounding dating involves deception. For instance, suppose a young man and woman would like to become better acquainted, but for a time they do not wish to make that widely known. Perhaps, as a young

> **TIP** ✔
>
> You don't have to broadcast your relationship around the globe. But do tell those who have a right to know. Most often, that includes your parents and the parents of the person you're dating.

man named Thomas says, "they don't want to be teased with questions like, 'So when are you getting married?'"

Undue pressure from others can indeed be harmful. (Song of Solomon 2:7) Therefore, at the initial stage of a relationship, some may well choose to be discreet. (Proverbs 10:19) "This gives two people time to decide if they're serious about each other," says 20-year-old Anna. "If they are, *then* they can go public."

At the same time, it would be wrong to hide your relationship from those who have a right to know about it, such as your parents or the parents of the person you're dating. Really, if you can't be open about your dating, you should ask yourself *why*. Do you know in your heart that your parents would have valid reason to object?

### "I Knew What I Had to Do"

Jessica, mentioned at the outset, changed her mind about secretly dating Jeremy when she heard the experi-

## ⟫⟫⟫ action plan!

*If I am dating a fellow Christian secretly, I will*

..................................................................................................

..................................................................................................

*If a friend of mine is dating secretly, I will*

..................................................................................................

..................................................................................................

*What I would like to ask my parent(s) about this subject is*

..................................................................................................

..................................................................................................

> **I stopped dating secretly. Yes, going back to school and seeing that boy every day was hard. But Jehovah God can see the bigger picture, whereas we can't. We just have to trust Jehovah.** —Jessica

ence of another Christian who was in a similar situation. "After hearing how she broke off the relationship," Jessica says, "I knew what I had to do." Was breaking up easy? No! "This was the only boy I had ever really liked," Jessica says. "I cried every day for several weeks."

Yet, Jessica knew that she loved Jehovah. And although she had become sidetracked, she truly wanted to do what was right. In time, the pain of breaking up subsided. "Now," Jessica says, "my relationship with Jehovah is better than ever. I'm so grateful that he gives us the direction we need at just the right time!"

**IN OUR NEXT CHAPTER** *You're ready to date, and you've found someone you like. But how do you know if this person is right for you?*

**WHAT DO YOU THINK?**

- Look back at the three situations highlighted in bold type on page 22. Which, if any, describes how *you* feel at times?

- How can you address the matter without dating secretly?

- If you knew that a friend was dating secretly, how would you deal with the situation, and why would you choose to do it that way?

**3**

# Is this person right for me?

**Take a moment to complete the following quiz:**

**What qualities would you currently view as essential in a potential marriage mate? In the list below, put a ✔ next to the four traits you feel are most important.**

✎ ❑ Good-looking ❑ Spiritually-minded
❑ Friendly ❑ Trustworthy
❑ Popular ❑ Morally upright
❑ Funny ❑ Goal-oriented

**When you were younger, did you ever develop a crush on anyone? In the list above, put an ✗ next to the one trait you found most appealing about that person at the time.**

THERE'S nothing wrong with *any* of the above traits. Each of them has its own appeal. Wouldn't you agree, though, that when you're in the grip of a youthful crush, you tend to dwell on the more superficial qualities, such as those in the left-hand column?

As you mature, however, you begin using your powers of perception to examine deeper issues, such as those in the right-hand column. For instance, you start to realize that the cutest girl in the neighborhood may not be all that trustworthy or that the most popular boy in class may not be morally upright. If you're past the bloom of youth, you most likely look beyond the superficial traits to answer the question, "Is this person right for me?"

## Know Yourself First

Before you can consider who might be right for you, you need to know yourself well. To learn more about yourself, answer the following questions:

What are my strengths?

..........................................................................

..........................................................................

What are my weaknesses or vulnerabilities?

..........................................................................

..........................................................................

What emotional and spiritual needs do I have?

..........................................................................

..........................................................................

Getting to know yourself is no small task, but questions like those above can get you started. The more you understand yourself, the better equipped you will be to find someone who will amplify your strengths rather than your weaknesses.* What if you think you've found that person?

## Will Just *Anyone* Do?

"Can I get to know you better?" That question will make you either cringe or leap for joy—depending on who's asking. Suppose you answer yes. Over the course of time, how can you tell if your boyfriend or girlfriend is right for *you*?

Suppose you want to buy a new pair of shoes. You go to the store and find a pair that catches your eye. You try on the shoes, only

* You can learn even more about yourself by considering the questions in Chapter 1 following the subheading "Are You Ready to Get Married?"

*Not just any size shoe will fit; similarly, not just anyone will make a good partner*

to find that—much to your disappointment—they're too tight. What would you do? Buy the shoes anyway? Or look for a different pair? Clearly, the better choice is to put the shoes back and look for others. It would make little sense to walk around in a pair of shoes that just didn't fit!

It's similar with choosing a marriage partner. Over time, more than a few members of the opposite sex may catch your eye. But not just anyone will do. After all, you want someone you'll be comfortable with—someone who truly fits your personality and your goals. (Genesis 2:18; Matthew 19:4-6) Have you found such a person? If so, how can you tell if that one is right for you?

## Looking Beyond the Surface

To answer that last question, look at your friend objectively. Be careful, though! You might be inclined to see only what you *want* to see. So take your time. Try to perceive your friend's true nature. This will take effort on your part. But that's only to be expected. To illustrate: Imagine that you want to purchase a car. How thoroughly would you research it? Would you be concerned only about the outer appearance? Wouldn't it make sense to look deeper—perhaps learning as much as you could about the condition of the engine?

*Do you think it's important to look beyond outward appearance when choosing a car? How much more so when choosing a marriage mate!*

Finding a mate is a much weightier issue than choosing a car. Yet, many who date don't look beyond the surface. Instead, they quickly point to the things they have in common: 'We like the same music.' 'We enjoy the same activities.' 'We agree on *everything!*' As mentioned earlier, though, if you're truly past the bloom of youth, you look beyond superficial traits. You see the need to discern "the secret person of the heart."—1 Peter 3:4; Ephesians 3:16.

For example, rather than focus on how much you *agree* on things, it might be more revealing to note what happens when you *disagree.* In other words, how does this person handle conflict—by insisting on his or her way, perhaps giving in to "fits of anger" or "abusive speech"? (Galatians 5:19, 20; Colossians 3:8) Or does this person show reasonableness—a willingness to yield for the sake of peace when no issue of right or wrong is at stake?—James 3:17.

Another factor to consider: Is the person manipulative, possessive, or jealous? Does he or she demand to know your every move? "I hear of dating couples who fight because one person can't stand that the other hasn't constantly 'checked in,'" says Nicole. "I think that's a bad sign."—1 Corinthians 13:4.

Issues such as those raised above focus on personality and conduct. However, it's just as important to learn something of your friend's reputation. How is that one viewed by others? You may want to talk to those who have known this

**TIP**

Engage in activities that reveal personal qualities:

● Study God's Word together.

● Observe each other participating at congregation meetings and in the ministry.

● Participate in Kingdom Hall cleaning and in building projects.

# The Shulammite

The young **Shulammite** woman knows she needs to keep a **clear head** in matters of romance. "I have put you under oath," she tells her companions, "that you try not to awaken or arouse love in me until it feels inclined." The Shulammite knows that **feelings** can quickly overpower reason. She realizes, for instance, that others could pressure her to yield to the advances of someone who isn't right for her. Even her own feelings could **cloud good judgment.** So the Shulammite remains like **"a wall."**—Song of Solomon 8:4, 10.

Is your view of love as mature as that of the Shulammite? Can you **listen to your head** and not just your heart? (Proverbs 2:10, 11) Sometimes others might try to **pressure you** into a relationship before you're ready for it. You might even bring such pressure upon yourself. For example, when you see a boy and girl walking hand in hand, do you feel **desperate** to have the same kind of relationship? Would you **settle** for someone who doesn't share your Bible-based beliefs? The Shulammite girl was **mature** when it came to matters of romance. You can be too!

## ›› "do not become unevenly yoked"

"Do not become unevenly yoked with unbelievers." That Bible principle, found at 2 Corinthians 6:14, likely makes sense to you. Still, you might find yourself drawn to an unbeliever. Why? Sometimes it's just physical attraction. "I would always see this girl in gym class," says a boy named Mark. "She would go out of her way to come up and talk to me. It was not hard for a friendship to develop."

If you know yourself and have confidence in your spiritual values—and if you're mature enough not to be ruled by your feelings—you'll know what you should do. Really, this person—no matter how attractive, charming, or seemingly virtuous—will *not* enhance your friendship with God.—James 4:4.

Of course, if a romance has developed, ending it won't be easy—something that a girl named Cindy found out. "I cried every day," she says. "I thought about the boy constantly, even during Christian meetings. I loved him so much that I thought I would rather die than lose him." Soon, though, Cindy saw the wisdom of her mother's counsel against dating an unbeliever. "It's good that I broke up with him," she says. "I have every confidence that Jehovah will provide for my needs."

Are you in a situation similar to that of Cindy? If so, you don't have to deal with it alone! You could talk to your parents. That's what Jim did when he found himself infatuated with a girl at school. "I finally asked my parents for help," he says. "This was a key to my overcoming these feelings." Congregation elders can also assist you. Why not talk to one of them about what you're going through? —Isaiah 32:1, 2.

person for some time, such as mature ones in the congregation. That way you will know if he or she is "well reported on."—Acts 16:1, 2.

It might be revealing to jot down your personal observations as to how your friend measures up in the areas discussed so far.

Personality ✎.................................................................

.................................................................................

Conduct .......................................................................

.................................................................................

Reputation ...................................................................

.................................................................................

You will also benefit by consulting the box "Would He Make a Good Husband for Me?" on page 39 or "Would She Make a Good Wife for Me?" on page 40. The questions raised will help you determine if your friend would make a suitable marriage partner.

What if after considering the matter, you conclude that this person may *not* be right for you? In that case, you're faced with the serious question:

## Should We Break Up?

Sometimes a breakup is a blessing. Consider the experience of Jill. "At first," she says, "I was flattered that my boyfriend was always worrying about where I was, what I was doing, and who I was with. But it got to the point where I couldn't spend time with anyone *but* him. He even got jealous when I spent time with my

**DID YOU KNOW . . .** ❓

**Research consistently shows that marriages between people of different religions are much more likely to end in divorce.**

> **"Even by his practices a boy makes himself recognized as to whether his activity is pure and upright."**
> —Proverbs 20:11.

• • • • • • • • •

family—especially my father. When I ended the relationship, I felt as if a huge weight had been lifted off my shoulders!"

Sarah had a similar experience. She began to notice that John, the young man she was dating, was sarcastic, demanding, and rude. "One time," Sarah recalls, "he came to the door three hours late! He ignored my mother when she answered the door, and then he said: 'Let's go. We're late.' Not 'I'm late,' but 'We're late.' He should have apologized or explained himself. Most of all, he should have shown my mother respect!" Of course, a single disappointing act or trait doesn't necessarily doom a relationship. (Psalm 130:3) But when Sarah realized that John's rudeness was a pattern rather than an isolated incident, she decided to end the relationship.

What if, like Jill and Sarah, you determine that the person you're dating wouldn't make a suitable marriage partner? In that case, *do not ignore your feelings!* Hard as it is to accept, it might be best to end the relationship. Proverbs 22:3 says: "Shrewd is the one that has seen the calamity and proceeds to conceal himself." If, for example, your friend exhibits one or more of the danger signs found on pages 39 and 40, it would be best to end the relationship—at least until the problem is corrected. True, breaking up may not be easy. But marriage is

READ MORE ABOUT THIS TOPIC IN VOLUME 1, CHAPTER 31

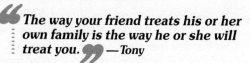

> **The way your friend treats his or her own family is the way he or she will treat you.** — *Tony*

a permanent bond. It's better to live with short-term pain now than suffer with lifelong regret later!

## Breaking the News

How should you go about breaking up? First, choose a proper setting for the discussion. What could that be? Well, think how *you* would like to be treated in such a situation. (Matthew 7:12) Would you want the announcement to be made in front of others? Likely not. Unless circumstances make it advisable, it would be best not to terminate a relationship by means of a telephone answering machine, a text message, or an e-mail. Instead, choose a time and place that will enable you to discuss this serious matter.

What should you say when the time comes to speak up? The apostle Paul urged Christians to "speak truth" with one another. (Ephesians 4:25) The best course, then, is to be tactful yet firm. State clearly why you feel that this relationship won't work *for you.* You don't need to recite a laundry list of faults or let loose with a barrage of criticism. In fact, instead of saying, *"You* don't" do this or *"You* never" do that, it would be better to use phrases that focus on how you feel— *"I* need a person who . . ."* or *"I feel that this relationship should end because . . ."*

This is no time to be wishy-washy or to yield to another's opinion. Remember, you have chosen to break up for a serious reason. So be cautious if your friend attempts to change your mind through subtle forms of manipulation. "After I ended the relationship," says a young woman named Lori, "my ex-boyfriend started acting depressed all the time. I think he did it to make me feel sorry for him. I did feel bad. But I didn't allow his reaction to alter my decision." Like Lori, know your own mind. Stick to your decision. Let your *no* mean no.—James 5:12.

## Aftermath of a Breakup

Don't be surprised if you're deeply upset for a time after the breakup. You might even feel like the psalmist who said: "I have become disconcerted, I have bowed low to an extreme degree; all day long I have walked about sad." (Psalm 38:6) Some well-intentioned friends may try to help by encouraging you to give the relationship another chance. Be careful! *You* will have to live with your decision—not your well-meaning friends. So don't be afraid to

### >>> action plan!

If I am attracted to an unbeliever, I will

...................................................................................

...................................................................................

To find out about the reputation of the person
I'm dating, I can

...................................................................................

...................................................................................

What I would like to ask my parent(s) about this
subject is

...................................................................................

...................................................................................

# would he make a good husband for me?

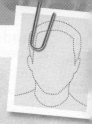

### character basics

☐ *How does he handle any authority he may have?*—Matthew 20:25, 26.

☐ *What are his goals?*—1 Timothy 4:15.

☐ *Is he **now** working toward those goals?*—1 Corinthians 9:26, 27.

☐ *How does he treat his family?*—Exodus 20:12.

☐ *Who are his friends?*—Proverbs 13:20.

☐ *What does he talk about?*—Luke 6:45.

☐ *What is his attitude toward money?*—Hebrews 13:5, 6.

☐ *What type of entertainment does he enjoy?*—Psalm 97:10.

☐ *How does he demonstrate his love for Jehovah?*—1 John 5:3.

### assets

☐ *Is he industrious?*—Proverbs 6:9-11.

☐ *Is he financially responsible?*—Luke 14:28.

☐ *Is he well reported on?*—Acts 16:1, 2.

☐ *Is he considerate of others?*—Philippians 2:4.

### danger signs

☐ *Is he disposed to anger?*—Proverbs 22:24.

☐ *Does he try to involve you in sexual misconduct?*—Galatians 5:19.

☐ *Is he physically or verbally abusive?*—Ephesians 4:31.

☐ *Does he need to use alcohol to have a good time?*—Proverbs 20:1.

☐ *Is he jealous and self-centered?*—1 Corinthians 13:4, 5.

# would she make a good wife for me?

### character basics

☐ How does she show submissiveness in the family and the congregation?
—Ephesians 5:21, 22.

☐ How does she treat her family?—Exodus 20:12.

☐ Who are her friends?—Proverbs 13:20.

☐ What does she talk about?—Luke 6:45.

☐ What is her attitude toward money?—1 John 2:15-17.

☐ What are her goals?—1 Timothy 4:15.

☐ Is she **now** working toward those goals?
—1 Corinthians 9:26, 27.

☐ What type of entertainment does she enjoy?—Psalm 97:10.

☐ How does she demonstrate her love for Jehovah?
—1 John 5:3.

### assets

☐ Is she industrious?—Proverbs 31:17, 19, 21, 22, 27.

☐ Is she financially responsible?—Proverbs 31:16, 18.

☐ Is she well reported on?—Ruth 3:11.

☐ Is she considerate of others?—Proverbs 31:20.

### danger signs

☐ Is she contentious?—Proverbs 21:19.

☐ Does she try to involve you in sexual misconduct?
—Galatians 5:19.

☐ Is she verbally or physically abusive?—Ephesians 4:31.

☐ Does she need to use alcohol to have a good time?
—Proverbs 20:1.

☐ Is she jealous and self-centered?—1 Corinthians 13:4, 5.

remain firm—even though you may feel sad about what's happened.

Be assured that, eventually, your painful feelings will pass. In the meantime, why not take positive steps, such as the following, to cope with the situation?

Express your feelings to a trusted confidant.* (Proverbs 15:22) Pray to Jehovah about the matter. (Psalm 55:22) Keep busy. (1 Corinthians 15:58) Don't become a loner! (Proverbs 18:1) Get right back into group association with those who will upbuild you. Strive to keep your mind on things that are positive.—Philippians 4:8.

In time, you may well find a new friend. No doubt you will do so with an even more balanced outlook. Perhaps this time your answer to the question "Is this person right for me?" will be *yes!*

---

* Your parents or other adults, such as Christian elders, can help. You might even find that they went through similar painful experiences when they were young.

**IN OUR NEXT CHAPTER** *Once you are dating, where should you draw the line when it comes to expressing your affection for each other?*

**WHAT DO YOU THINK?**

- What positive qualities would you bring into a marriage relationship?

- What vital qualities would you look for in a marriage partner?

- What complex issues could arise if you were to marry someone who didn't share your faith?

- In what ways could you learn of the character, conduct, and reputation of someone you're dating?

# 4

# How far is too far?

*True or false . . .*

*It's always wrong for two people who are dating to touch each other, under any circumstances.*  ☐ True  ☐ False

*A couple who refrain from sexual intercourse can still be guilty of fornication.*  ☐ True  ☐ False

*If a dating couple don't take sexual liberties, they can't really be in love.*  ☐ True  ☐ False

NO DOUBT you've thought about this subject a lot. After all, if you're dating someone, it can be difficult to know where to draw the line when expressing affection. Let's address the three true-or-false statements above and see how God's Word helps us to answer the question, "How far is too far?"

● **It's always wrong for two people who are dating to touch each other, under any circumstances.**

**False.** The Bible doesn't condemn legitimate, clean expressions of affection. For example, the Bible tells the story of a Shulammite girl and a shepherd boy who were in love. Their courtship was chaste. Yet, they evidently exchanged *some* displays of affection before they married. (Song of Solomon 1:2; 2:6; 8:5) Today some couples who are seriously contemplating marriage may likewise feel that some chaste expressions of affection are appropriate.*

However, a dating couple must exercise extreme caution. Kissing, embracing, or doing anything that causes arousal can lead to sexual misconduct. It's all too easy, even for a couple with honorable intentions, to get carried away and engage in sexual immorality.—Colossians 3:5.

● **A couple who refrain from sexual intercourse can still be guilty of fornication.**

**True.** The original Greek word translated "fornication" (*por·nei′a*) has a broad meaning. It describes all forms of sexual relations outside of marriage and focuses on the misuse of the sexual organs. Thus, fornication includes not only intercourse but also acts such as masturbating another person, as well as engaging in oral sex or anal sex.

**DID YOU KNOW . . .**

If you're engaged, you need to discuss some intimate matters. But explicit talk that's intended to arouse sexual desire is a form of uncleanness—even if it's carried on over the phone or via text messaging.

---

* In some parts of the world, public displays of affection between unmarried individuals are considered to be in poor taste and offensive. Christians take care not to behave in a way that could stumble others. —2 Corinthians 6:3.

## ⋗ what if we've gone too far?

**What if you've fallen into improper conduct? Don't deceive yourself into thinking you can solve the problem alone. "I'd pray, 'Help us not to do it again,'" confessed one youth. "Sometimes it would work, but a few times it didn't." Therefore, talk to your parents. The Bible also gives this good advice: "Call the older men of the congregation." (James 5:14) These Christian shepherds can give counsel, advice, and reproof so that you can get your relationship with God back on track.**

Furthermore, the Bible condemns more than just fornication. The apostle Paul wrote: "The works of the flesh are manifest, and they are fornication, uncleanness, loose conduct." He added: "Those who practice such things will not inherit God's kingdom."—Galatians 5:19-21.

What is "uncleanness"? The Greek word covers impurity of any kind, in speech or action. Surely it would be unclean to allow one's hands to stray under another person's clothing, to remove another's clothing, or to caress another's intimate areas, such as the breasts. In the Bible the caressing of the breasts is associated with the pleasures reserved for married couples.—Proverbs 5:18, 19.

Some youths brazenly defy godly standards. They *deliberately* go too far, or they greedily seek out numerous partners with whom they can practice sexual uncleanness. Such ones may be guilty of what the apostle Paul called "loose conduct." The Greek word for "loose conduct" means 'outrageous acts, excess, insolence, unbridled lust.' Surely you want to avoid coming to be "past all moral sense" by giving yourself over to "loose conduct to work

READ MORE ABOUT THIS TOPIC IN VOLUME 1, CHAPTER 24

**"Love . . . does not behave indecently."**
—1 Corinthians 13:4, 5.

• • • • • • • • •

uncleanness of every sort with greediness."—Ephesians 4:17-19.

● *If a dating couple don't take sexual liberties, they can't really be in love.*

**False.** Contrary to what some may think, taking improper sexual liberties doesn't deepen a relationship. Rather, it tears down mutual respect and trust. Consider Laura's experience. "One day my boyfriend came over when my mother wasn't home, supposedly just to watch TV," she says. "At first he just held my hand. Then all of a sudden, his hands started to wander. I was afraid to tell him to stop; I thought he would get upset and want to leave."

What do you think? Did Laura's boyfriend really care for her, or was he just seeking selfish gratification? Is someone who tries to draw you into unclean behavior really showing that he loves you?

When a boy pressures a girl into violating her Christian training and conscience, he breaks God's law and undermines any claim that he genuinely loves her. Furthermore, a girl who willingly gives in allows herself to be exploited. Worse yet, she has committed an unclean act—perhaps even fornication.*—1 Corinthians 6:9, 10.

> **TIP** ✔
>
> **Date in groups, or insist on having a chaperone. Avoid risky settings, such as being alone in a parked car or in a house or an apartment.**

_____

\* Of course, the issues raised in this paragraph apply to both genders.

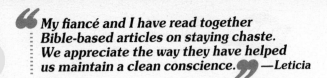

*My fiancé and I have read together Bible-based articles on staying chaste. We appreciate the way they have helped us maintain a clean conscience.* —Leticia

### Set Clear Boundaries

If you're dating, how can you avoid inappropriate displays of affection? The wise course is to *set clear boundaries in advance.* Proverbs 13:10 says: "With those consulting together there is wisdom." So discuss with your partner what expressions of affection are appropriate. Waiting until you're in some emotion-charged romantic setting before establishing ground rules is like waiting until your house is on fire before installing an alarm.

Granted, such a sensitive discussion can be difficult —even embarrassing—especially in the early stages of courtship. But establishing boundaries can do much to prevent serious problems from developing later on. Wise

### ⟩⟩⟩ action plan!

*I can avoid being tempted to toy with immorality by*

.............................................................................................

.............................................................................................

*If the person I'm dating tries to pressure me into unclean conduct, I will*

.............................................................................................

.............................................................................................

*What I would like to ask my parent(s) about this subject is*

.............................................................................................

.............................................................................................

*Would you wait until your house caught fire before you installed an alarm? Then don't wait until your passions are aroused before you establish ground rules for conduct*

boundaries can be like smoke detectors that sound an alarm at the first hint of fire. Furthermore, your ability to communicate in these matters may also serve as an indicator of how much potential the relationship has. In fact, self-control, patience, and unselfishness are the foundation of a satisfying sexual relationship in marriage.—1 Corinthians 7:3, 4.

True, holding to godly standards isn't easy. But you can trust Jehovah's advice. After all, at Isaiah 48:17, he describes himself as "the One teaching you to benefit yourself, the One causing you to tread in the way in which you should walk." Jehovah has your best interests at heart!

**IN OUR NEXT CHAPTER** *Virginity doesn't make you abnormal. On the contrary, it's the wise course. Find out why.*

### WHAT DO YOU THINK?

- What limits would you set on physical contact with a member of the opposite sex?

- Explain how fornication, uncleanness, and loose conduct differ.

**5**

# Why stay a virgin?

*"I feel pressure to experiment with sex."—Kelly.*

*"I feel strange for still being a virgin."—Jordon.*

"ARE you *still* a virgin?" The very question might make you cower! After all, in many places a youth who is a virgin is likely to be viewed as a curiosity, an oddball. No wonder so many young people have sex before they're out of their teens!

## Pulled by Desire, Pushed by Peers

If you are a Christian, you know that the Bible tells you to "abstain from fornication." (1 Thessalonians 4:3) Still, you might find it hard to control your sexual urges. "At

## ❖ what *really* happens next?

Your peers and popular entertainment often cleverly mask the unpleasant realities of premarital sex. Look at the following three scenarios. What do you think would *really* happen to these teens?

● A schoolmate brags that he's had sex with many girls. He says it's fun—nobody gets hurt. What *really* happens next—to him *and* to the girls? ✎ ..............................

...................................................................................

● A movie ends with two unmarried teens having sex as a way to express their love for each other. What would happen next—in real life? ...................................

...................................................................................

● You meet a cute boy who asks you for sex. He says no one has to find out about it. If you gave in and tried to cover it up, what would *really* happen next? ......................

...................................................................................

times, thoughts about sex enter my mind without any apparent cause or reason," admits a young man named Paul. Be assured that to a large extent, such feelings are normal.

However, being the victim of unrelenting teasing and harassment for being a virgin is no fun at all! For instance, what if your peers tell you that you're not a real man or woman unless you've had sex? "Your peers make sex seem exciting and normal," says Ellen. "If you're not sleeping around, you're classed as weird."

But there's a side to premarital sex that your peers may not talk about. For example, Maria, who had sex with

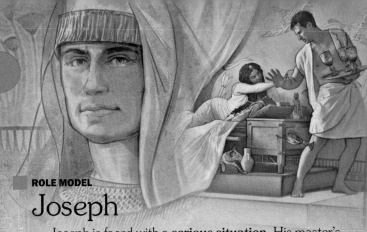

# Joseph

Joseph is faced with a **serious situation.** His master's wife has repeatedly implored him to have sex with her. Now she's trying again! But Joseph isn't tempted. In fact, his **reply is resolute.** "How could I commit this great badness and actually **sin against God?**" he says to her. When she challenges his refusal—even grabbing hold of him—Joseph isn't embarrassed to flee. In fact, **he runs** out of the house! Joseph shows himself to be a man of **moral integrity.**—Genesis 39:7-12.

You too may be confronted with a situation in which someone wants you to give in to your sexual urges. Resisting isn't merely a matter of willpower. It starts with a desire to **please your Creator,** Jehovah God. You see, Joseph had sexual desires, just as you do. However, it was unthinkable for him to satisfy those urges in a way that would offend his Creator. In the same way, you need to **be convinced** that moral uncleanness offends God and that it ultimately leads to heartache. So strive to **develop and maintain** the moral integrity that Joseph displayed.

her boyfriend, recalls: "Afterwards I felt embarrassed and ashamed. I hated myself and I hated my boyfriend." Such experiences are more typical than most youths realize. In reality, premarital sex is often an emotionally painful experience—with devastating consequences!

However, a youth named Shanda asks, "Why would God give young people sexual desires, knowing that they should not use them until after marriage?" That's a good question. But consider the following:

*Are sexual urges the only strong feelings you experience?* Not at all. Jehovah God created you with the capacity to feel a wide range of desires and emotions.

*Do you have to act on each impulse the instant that it wells up inside you?* No, for God also made you with the ability to control your actions.

What's the lesson, then? You may not be able to keep certain desires from arising, but you *can* control your reaction to them. Really, to act upon *every* sexual urge would be as wrong and foolish as hitting someone each time you felt anger.

The fact is, God never intended for us to misuse our procreative powers. "Each one

**DID YOU KNOW...**

Sexually permissive people are unlikely to change their habits just because they get married. In contrast, those who are loyal to God's moral standards before marriage are more likely to be loyal to their mate afterward.

of you should know how to get possession of his own vessel in sanctification and honor," says the Bible. (1 Thessalonians 4:4) Just as there is "a time to love and a time to hate," there is also a time to act on sexual urges and a time to refrain from doing so. (Ecclesiastes 3:1-8) Ultimately, *you* are in control of your desires!

But what can you do if someone taunts you, saying with disbelief, "Are you *really* still a virgin?" Don't be intimidated. To a person who only wants to put you down, you could say: "Yes, I *am* still a virgin, and you know what? I'm glad I am!" Or you could say, "That is a personal matter I don't discuss with others."* (Proverbs 26:4; Colossians 4:6) On the other hand, you might feel that the person questioning you deserves to know more. In that case you may well choose to explain your Bible-based stand.

✔ **TIP**

Avoid association with those who lack strong moral standards, even if they claim to share your religious beliefs.

Can you think of some other replies to the taunt "Are you *really* still a virgin?" If so, write them below.

✎ ......................................................................................

......................................................................................

**A Precious Gift**

How does God feel when people decide to have sex before marriage? Well, imagine that you've purchased a gift for a friend. But before you can give it to that friend, he or she—out of sheer curiosity—opens the gift! Wouldn't you be upset? Imagine, then, how God would feel if you were

---

\* Interestingly, Jesus chose to remain silent when questioned by Herod. (Luke 23:8, 9) Silence is often a good way to handle impertinent questions.

READ MORE ABOUT THIS TOPIC IN VOLUME 1, CHAPTER 23

> **"If anyone . . . has made this decision in his own heart, to keep his own virginity, he will do well."**
> —1 Corinthians 7:37.

• • • • • • • •

to engage in premarital sex. He wants you to wait until you're married to enjoy the gift of sexual relations.—Genesis 1:28.

What should you do about your sexual feelings? Put simply, learn to control them. You have the strength to do so! Pray to Jehovah to help you. His spirit can enhance your ability to exercise self-control. (Galatians 5:22, 23) Remind yourself that Jehovah "will not hold back anything good from those walking in faultlessness." (Psalm 84:11) Says a youth named Gordon: "When I find myself thinking

## ▶▶▶ *action plan!*

*If I am going to stay a virgin until I'm married, I will need to*

✎ ..........................................................................

..........................................................................

*If my associates are making it difficult for me to keep my resolve, I will*

..........................................................................

..........................................................................

*What I would like to ask my parent(s) about this subject is*

..........................................................................

..........................................................................

*Engaging in premarital sex is like opening a gift before it has been given to you*

that premarital sex would not be so bad, I reflect on the bad *spiritual* consequences and realize that no sin is worth the loss of my relationship with Jehovah."

The fact is, virginity is *not* strange or abnormal. It's immoral sex that is degrading, humiliating, and harmful. So don't let the world's propaganda con you into thinking that something is wrong with you if you hold to Bible standards. By retaining your virginity, you protect your health, your emotional well-being, and—most important of all—your relationship with God.

**WHAT DO YOU THINK?**

- Why in your opinion do some ridicule those who are virgins?
- Why can it be difficult to remain a virgin?
- What are the benefits of remaining a virgin until you're married?
- How would you explain the benefits of virginity to a younger sibling?

*my journal*

*If you're interested in getting married, write down the two most important attributes you would look for in a marriage mate and explain why you value those qualities. If you prefer to remain single, at least for a time, write about two advantages of singleness.*

# LIFE CHANGES 2

*Are you unhappy with the way your body is developing?* ❏ Yes ❏ No

*Have the changes of puberty left you feeling alone, confused, or afraid?* ❏ Yes ❏ No

*Do thoughts about the opposite sex tend to consume your waking hours?* ❏ Yes ❏ No

If you checked "yes" in response to any of the above questions, relax—it doesn't mean there's anything wrong with you! The fact is, the physical and emotional changes of adolescence can leave you feeling ecstatic and depressed and every emotion in between. Sure, you always wanted to be an adult, but now that the process has begun, it can be scary! **Chapters 6-8** will help you deal with life changes.

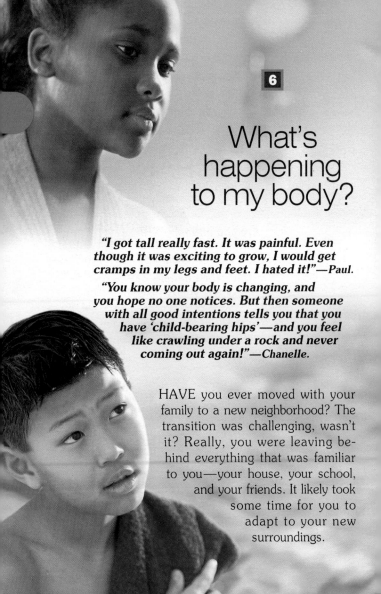

# 6

# What's happening to my body?

*"I got tall really fast. It was painful. Even though it was exciting to grow, I would get cramps in my legs and feet. I hated it!"*—Paul.

*"You know your body is changing, and you hope no one notices. But then someone with all good intentions tells you that you have 'child-bearing hips'—and you feel like crawling under a rock and never coming out again!"*—Chanelle.

HAVE you ever moved with your family to a new neighborhood? The transition was challenging, wasn't it? Really, you were leaving behind everything that was familiar to you—your house, your school, and your friends. It likely took some time for you to adapt to your new surroundings.

At the onset of puberty—the stage of life in which you become physically mature—you enter one of life's greatest transitions. In a sense, you're moving to a whole new "neighborhood." Exciting? Absolutely! But the move to adulthood can elicit mixed feelings, and it may not be easy for you to adapt. What happens during this thrilling yet turbulent time in your life?

## Just for Girls

Adolescence is a time of dramatic transition. Some of the changes you'll experience will be quite visible. For example, hormones trigger the growth of hair in your genital area. Also, you'll notice growth of your breasts, hips, thighs, and buttocks. Your body is slowly leaving behind the silhouette of a child and adopting the feminine curves of an adult. This is nothing to be alarmed about—it's perfectly normal. And it's evidence that your body is preparing itself for the time when you'll be able to pass on life through childbirth!

Some time after puberty begins, you'll experience the beginning of the menstrual cycle. Without adequate preparation, this milestone in your life could be frightening. "I was totally caught off guard when I started getting my period," recalls Samantha. "I felt dirty. I would scrub myself down in the shower and think 'I'm so gross.' The thought of getting a period every month for years to come terrified me!"

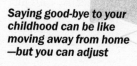

*Saying good-bye to your childhood can be like moving away from home—but you can adjust*

Remember, though, that the menstrual cycle is evidence that your reproductive powers are developing. Even though it will be years before you're ready to be a parent, here you stand poised on the brink of womanhood. Still, the onset of menstruation can be unsettling. "The worst thing I had to deal with was the emotional mood swings," says Kelli. "It was so frustrating not knowing how I could be so happy all day but then be crying my eyes out that same night."

**DID YOU KNOW . . .**

Puberty can begin as early as age eight or as late as the mid-teens. There's a wide range as to what's normal.

If that's the way you feel right now, be patient. In time you'll adjust. Says 20-year-old Annette: "I remember when I came to the point of accepting that this was what was going to make me a woman and that Jehovah gave me the gift to bear life. That takes a while to accept, and it's really hard for some girls; but in time you learn to accept the changes."

Have you started to experience some of the physical changes discussed above? On the following lines, write down any questions you have about the changes you are experiencing. ✎ ...............................................................

............................................................................................

............................................................................................

## Just for Boys

If you're a boy, puberty will have a profound effect upon your appearance. For example, your skin might frequently become oily, resulting in pimples and blackheads.* "It's just irritating and frustrating to have all these pimples come

---

* Girls experience this as well. The problem can usually be kept in check with good skin care.

> **There are many insecurities that come with adolescence, and you're never really sure where your body is going to go next. But as you grow, you learn to accept the changes and even embrace them.** —*Annette*

out," says 18-year-old Matt. "It's a full-fledged war—you have to fight against them. You don't know if they'll ever go away or if they'll leave scars or if people will think less of you because you have them."

On the plus side, though, you may notice that you are becoming bigger and stronger and that your shoulders are starting to broaden. Also during puberty, hair may grow on your legs, chest, and face, as well as under your arms. By the way, the amount of body hair you have has nothing to do with how manly you are; it's simply a matter of heredity.

Since not all parts of your body grow at the same rate, you may experience a degree of clumsiness at this stage. "I was as graceful as a giraffe on roller skates," recalls Dwayne. "It seemed as if my brain would send out a command, and my limbs would receive it a week later!"

During the mid-teens your voice deepens, but the process is gradual. For a time, rich, deep tones may be suddenly interrupted by humiliating cracks and squeaks. Don't worry, though. Eventually, your voice will smooth out. In the meantime, learning to laugh at yourself will help minimize the embarrassment.

**TIP** ✔

As your body begins to develop, take care to avoid styles of clothing that are provocative. Always dress "with modesty and soundness of mind." —1 Timothy 2:9.

> **"I shall laud you because in a fear-inspiring way I am wonderfully made."**—Psalm 139:14.

• • • • • • • • •

As your reproductive system matures, your sexual organs will enlarge and hair will grow around them. They will also begin to manufacture semen. This fluid contains millions of microscopic sperm, which are released during sexual intercourse. A sperm is capable of fertilizing a female egg and producing a baby.

Semen builds up in your body. Some is absorbed, but from time to time, some may be released at night while you sleep. This is commonly called a wet dream. Such emissions are normal. Even the Bible makes mention of them. (Leviticus 15:16, 17) They indicate that your reproductive system is functioning and that you're on your way to manhood.

Have you started to experience some of the physical changes discussed above? On the following lines, write down any questions you have about the changes you are experiencing. ✎ .................................................................

.......................................................................................

.......................................................................................

## Coping With New Feelings

As the reproductive system matures, both boys and girls become aware of the opposite sex as never before. "When I hit puberty, I suddenly realized how many pretty girls there were," says Matt. "That was really frustrating, because I also realized that I couldn't do anything about it until I was much older." Chapter 29 of this book will discuss in greater detail this aspect of growing up. For now, though,

# how can I talk to dad or mom about sex?

*"If I had a question about sex, I wouldn't ask my parents."—Beth.*

*"I wouldn't have the guts to bring it up."—Dennis.*

If you're like Beth or Dennis, you're in a dilemma. You want to know about sex, but the people who have the answers may be the ones you're least inclined to ask —your parents! You worry about many things:

## What will they think of me?

*"I wouldn't want them to be suspicious of me because I'm asking."—Jessica.*

*"They want you to stay young and innocent forever, and the day you start talking to them about sex, you lose that to a degree."—Beth.*

## How will they react?

*"I'd be afraid that my parents would jump to conclusions before I finished speaking and launch into a long lecture."—Gloria.*

*"My parents aren't very good at hiding their feelings, so I'd be afraid of seeing a facial expression of disappointment. In fact, my dad would probably be thinking up a lecture while I was speaking."—Pam.*

## Will they misinterpret my reason for asking?

*"They might overreact and start asking questions like, 'Have you been tempted to have sex?' or 'Are your peers pressuring you?' But maybe you're just curious."—Lisa.*

*"My dad always gets this worried expression when I mention a guy. Then he goes right into the sex talk. I'm thinking, 'Dad, I just said he was cute. I didn't say anything about marriage or sex!' "—Stacey.*

If it's any comfort, your parents may feel as awkward talking to *you* about sex as you would feel talking to *them!* Perhaps that explains the findings of one survey in which 65 percent of parents reported talking to their children about sex, but only 41 percent of the children could recall having such a discussion.

The fact is, your parents may be hesitant to talk about sex. In many cases their parents simply didn't talk about it to them! Whatever the reason, cut your parents a little slack. Maybe—in a bold move that will benefit both you and them—*you* can bring it up. How?

## Broaching the Subject

Your parents have a wealth of wisdom and advice on the matter of sex. You just need a key to open a discussion. Try the following:

1  State your fear outright, thus getting it out in the open. *"I'm a little hesitant to bring this up because I'm afraid that you might think . . ."*

2  Then tell your parent why you've come to him or her. *"But I have a question, and I'd rather have you answer it than anyone else."*

3  Then just state the issue. *"My question is . . ."*

4  At the end of the discussion, make sure the door is open to talk again in the future. *"If anything else comes to my mind, can I talk to you about this again?"*

Even if you know the answer will be yes, hearing your parent *say* it will keep the door open and make you feel more comfortable the next time you need to talk. So try it out! You may end up agreeing with Trina. Now 24, she says: "At the time my mom and I were talking, I remember wishing that we weren't having the discussion at all. But now I'm glad my mom was so frank and open. It's been a real protection!"

you should realize that it's important that you learn to control your sexual urges. (Colossians 3:5) As difficult as it may seem, you *can* choose not to act on them!

There are other feelings that you may have to cope with during puberty. For example, it's easy to feel bad about yourself. Loneliness is common among young people, and so are bouts of the blues. At such times, it's good to talk to a parent or other trustworthy adult. Write the name of an adult *you* could talk to about your feelings.

✎ .........................................................................................................

**The Most Important Growth**

Your most important growth involves, not your height, shape, or facial features, but your development as a person —mentally, emotionally and, above all, spiritually. Said the apostle Paul: "When I was a babe, I used to speak as a babe, to think as a babe, to reason as a babe; but now that I have become a man, I have done away with the traits of a babe." (1 Corinthians 13:11) The lesson is clear. It's not enough to

### ▶▶▶ action plan!

*As I progress toward adulthood, the trait I need to work on most is*

✎ .........................................................................................................

*To take care of my spiritual growth, I will*

.........................................................................................................

.........................................................................................................

*What I would like to ask my parent(s) about this subject is*

.........................................................................................................

.........................................................................................................

look like an adult. You must learn to act, speak, and think like an adult. Don't become so concerned about what's happening to your body that you neglect to take care of the inner person!

Remember, too, that God "sees what the heart is." (1 Samuel 16:7) The Bible says that King Saul was tall and handsome, but he was a failure both as a king and as a man. (1 Samuel 9:2) In contrast, Zacchaeus was "small in size," yet he had the inner strength to turn his life around and become a disciple of Jesus. (Luke 19:2-10) Clearly, what's on the *inside* is what counts most.

One thing is sure: There's no safe way either to speed up or to delay the process of physically growing up. So instead of greeting the changes with hostility and fear, accept them graciously—and with a sense of humor. Puberty isn't a disease, nor are you the first one to go through it. And rest assured, you *will* survive. When the storm of puberty is over, you will emerge as a full-grown adult!

**IN OUR NEXT CHAPTER** *What if you don't like what you see when you look in the mirror? How can you have a balanced view of your appearance?*

---

**WHAT DO YOU THINK?**

- Why are the physical and emotional changes of puberty so difficult to deal with?

- What do you find most challenging about this transition?

- Why might your love for God tend to diminish during puberty, but how can you prevent that from happening?

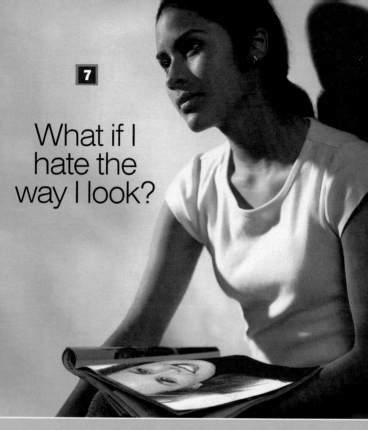

**7**

# What if I
# hate the
# way I look?

*Are you often disappointed*
*with the way you look?*  ☐ Yes  ☐ No

*Have you ever considered*
*resorting to cosmetic surgery*
*or an extreme diet to correct*
*a physical flaw?*  ☐ Yes  ☐ No

*What physical feature(s) would*   Height      Weight
*you change about yourself if you*   Body shape   Hair
*could? (Circle those that apply.)*   Complexion   Voice

IF YOU answered yes to the first two questions and circled three or more features in the third, consider the bright side of the situation: There's a good chance that others don't see you as negatively as you see yourself. It's easy to go overboard and worry about your appearance too much. In fact, one poll revealed that young women are often more afraid of putting on pounds than they are of nuclear war, of cancer, or even of losing their parents!

There's no doubt that how you look can affect how you view yourself—and how you're treated by others. "Growing-ing up, my two older sisters were completely gorgeous, and I was the chubby one," says 19-year-old Maritza. "I received plenty of ridicule in school. On top of that, my aunt nicknamed me Chubs, which was the name of her small and overweight dog!" Julie, 16, had a similar experience. "A girl at school teased me and said I had 'bunny teeth.' Even though it wasn't a big deal, it still made me feel bad, and even now I'm uncomfortable with my teeth!"

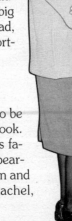

*Your perception of yourself can be just like the reflection in a distorted mirror*

## Concern or Obsession—Which?

It's not wrong for you to be concerned about how you look. In fact, the Bible comments favorably on the physical appearance of a number of women and men, including Sarah, Rachel,

> **For a long time, I was teased about how big my eyes are. I learned to laugh but also to be confident in my personality and other strengths. I've come to terms with my appearance. I accept myself as I am.** —Amber

Joseph, David, and Abigail. The Bible says that a woman named Abishag was "beautiful in the extreme."—1 Kings 1:4.

However, many youths are *obsessed* with their appearance. Some girls, for example, believe that being attractive means being *thin,* and those superslim models in the slick magazine ads certainly seem to support that belief. Never mind that those stunning photos were airbrushed to perfection or enhanced on a computer and that those lithe specimens have to keep themselves in a state of near starvation to maintain their figure! Still, comparing yourself with what you see in magazines might leave you distraught. What if you're genuinely unhappy about your appearance? First, you need to take a realistic look at yourself.

## A Distorted Image?

Have you ever looked at yourself in a distorted mirror? The reflection might make you look bigger or smaller than you actually are. Either way, the view is inaccurate.

Similarly, many youths have a distorted self-image. Consider this: In one study, 58 percent of

**DID YOU KNOW . . .**

Some experts warn that if you starve yourself to shed pounds, your body may shift into "crisis mode," slow down your metabolism, and quickly cause you to regain any weight you've lost!

girls claimed to be overweight, when, in fact, only 17 percent were. In another study, 45 percent of women who were actually *underweight* thought that they were too heavy!

Some researchers say that most girls who are worried about their weight have no reason to be. That fact may provide little comfort, of course, if you truly have a stocky frame. If that's so in your case, what could be the cause?

Genes could play a role. Some people are thin and angular by nature. But if your genes have designated you to have a rounder figure and more body fat, you were simply not programmed to be thin. Even at your medically ideal weight, you'll probably look heavier than you prefer. Exercise and diet can help, yet for the most part, you're stuck with your inherited body shape.

Another factor could be the normal changes of adolescence. At puberty a girl goes from having about 8 percent body fat to about 22 percent body fat. Often, such a situation changes over time, and a plump 11- or 12-year-old girl will emerge from puberty as a shapely teenager. On the other hand, what if your physique is the result of poor nutrition or a lack of exercise? What if you really need to lose weight for legitimate health reasons?

> **TIP**
>
> When you're trying to lose weight . . .
>
> ● Don't skip breakfast. If you do, the resulting hunger may actually cause you to eat *more* than you would otherwise.
>
> ● Drink a large glass of water before each meal. It will curb your appetite and help you control how much you eat.

### A Balanced Approach

The Bible speaks highly of being "moderate in habits." (1 Timothy 3:11) So avoid skipping meals or going to ex-

READ MORE ABOUT THIS TOPIC IN VOLUME 1, CHAPTER 10

**"Man sees what appears to the eyes; but as for Jehovah, he sees what the heart is."**—1 Samuel 16:7.

• • • • • • • • •

tremes in dieting. Perhaps the best way to shed pounds is to adopt a plan of healthful eating and get a reasonable amount of exercise.

There's no need to resort to a fad diet. For example, diet pills may curb your appetite for a while; but the body quickly adjusts to them, and your appetite returns. Or your metabolism slows down, and you gain weight anyway—not to mention the side effects some experience, such as dizziness, high blood pressure, anxiety attacks, and perhaps even addiction. Much the same can be said for pills that eliminate water or that speed up your metabolism.

In contrast, a reasonable eating program, balanced with moderate but regular exercise, will help you look and feel your best. Moderate aerobics several times a week will work wonders for your health. Something as simple as a brisk walk or stair climbing may suffice.

### Beware of the Anorexia Trap!

In their quest to lose weight, some youths have fallen victim to anorexia—a life-threatening eating disorder that really amounts to self-starvation. Says Masami, after some four months of getting help for her anorexia: "When people tell me 'you look well,' I say to myself, 'It must be because I'm getting fat.' At times like that, I cry to myself and I think, 'If only I could go back to my previous weight —the weight I was four months ago!'"

Anorexia can develop innocently. A young girl might embark on a seemingly harmless diet, perhaps to lose just a few pounds. When she reaches her goal, however, she isn't content. "I'm still too fat!" she declares as she stares disapprovingly at herself in the mirror. So she decides to lose just a few more pounds. Then just a few more. And a few more. The pattern is set, and the seeds of anorexia are sown.

If you have symptoms of anorexia or any other eating disorder, *you need to get help.* Confide in a parent or another trusted adult. A Bible proverb states: "A true companion is loving all the time, and is a brother that is born for when there is distress."—Proverbs 17:17.

### Defining True Beauty

On the whole, the Bible places very little emphasis on one's physical appearance or bodily shape. Rather, it's the inner person that truly makes one either attractive or not in the eyes of God.—Proverbs 11:20, 22.

### >>> action plan!

*I can take better care of my health by*

..............................................................................................................

..............................................................................................................

*For me, a reasonable program of exercise would include*

..............................................................................................................

..............................................................................................................

*What I would like to ask my parent(s) about this subject is*

..............................................................................................................

..............................................................................................................

Consider King David's son Absalom. The Bible says: "There proved to be no man so beautiful in all Israel as to be praised so much. From the sole of his foot to the crown of his head there proved to be no defect in him." (2 Samuel 14:25) Yet, this young man was treacherous. Pride and ambition impelled him to try to usurp the throne of Jehovah's appointed king. The Bible, therefore, doesn't paint a pretty picture of Absalom but, rather, portrays him as a man of shameless disloyalty and murderous hatred.

The bottom line is that "Jehovah is making an estimate of hearts"—not the size of a girl's waistline or a boy's biceps. (Proverbs 21:2) So while there's nothing wrong with wanting to look good, far more important than your appearance is your personality. In the long run, spiritual qualities will make you more attractive to others than chiseled muscles or a flat stomach!

**IN OUR NEXT CHAPTER** *Many youths are afflicted with a chronic illness or disability. If that's true of you, how can you cope with your situation?*

**WHAT DO YOU THINK?**

- How do you feel about the way you look?
- What are some reasonable steps you can take to improve your appearance?
- What would you say to a friend who has developed an eating disorder?
- How would you help a younger sibling acquire a balanced view of his or her appearance?

**8**

# Why do I have to be so sick?

*"When you are young, you feel invincible. Then, suddenly, being seriously ill shakes you out of that. You feel that you have become old overnight."—Jason.*

AT 18 years of age, Jason learned that he had Crohn's disease, a debilitating and painful bowel disorder. Perhaps you too suffer from a chronic illness or disability. Activities that many take for granted—including getting dressed, eating, or going to school—might require enormous amounts of effort.

A chronic health problem can make you feel as though you're locked in a prison, with your freedom restricted. You may feel lonely. You might even start to wonder if you've done something to offend God or if God has brought some special test of integrity upon you. However, the

(Continued on page 79)

*A chronic health problem can make you feel as though you're locked in a prison—but the Bible provides hope of a release*

■ **DUSTIN, 22** 66 *I remember crying in my mother's arms when I learned that I would be confined to a wheelchair. I was only eight years old.*

*I have muscular dystrophy. I need help getting dressed, showered, and fed. I can't lift my arms at all. Still, my life has been busy and enjoyable, and I have much to be grateful for. I go out in the ministry regularly and serve as a ministerial servant in the congregation. It doesn't even occur to me that I need to 'cope.' In serving Jehovah, there's always something to do and to look forward to. Ultimately, I look forward to God's new world, where I will 'climb up just as a stag does.'* 99 —Isaiah 35:6.

■ **TOMOKO, 21** 66 *When I was just four years old, the doctor told me: 'You'll have to take insulin injections for the rest of your life.'*

*Controlling blood sugar levels is challenging for a diabetic. Often, I can't eat when I want to, and when I don't want to eat, I have to. To date, I've had about 25,000 injections, so I have calluses on my arms and thighs. But my parents have helped me to make the best of my situation. They were always cheerful and positive, and they raised me to appreciate spiritual things. Jehovah has been good to me. When my health allowed it, I decided to show my appreciation by taking up the full-time ministry.* 99

■ **JAMES, 18** **❝People don't know how to respond to someone who's out of the ordinary, and that's just what I am.**

I have a rare form of dwarfism. People put a lot of emphasis on appearance, so I'm always trying to prove that I'm not a little child with a deep voice. Rather than mope over what I'm not, I try to focus on what I am. I enjoy my life. I study the Bible and pray to Jehovah for support. My family is always there to encourage me. I look forward to the time when God will eliminate all ailments. In the meantime, I live with my disability, but I don't let my disability become my life.❞

■ **DANITRIA, 16** **❝I knew that something was wrong when even picking up a simple glass of water hurt so much.**

Having fibromyalgia is a pain, literally and figuratively. As a teen, I want to keep up with my friends, but everything is more difficult for me than it used to be. Even falling asleep seems to take forever! Still, I've learned that with

Jehovah's help I can work around my problem. I was even able to spend extra time in the ministry as an auxiliary pioneer. It was hard, but I did it. I try to do my best. I have to 'listen' to my body and stay within my limits. If I forget, I've always got my mom to remind me!❞

**ELYSIA, 20** **"I used to be an A-plus student. Now reading a simple sentence is a challenge, and that sometimes makes me feel depressed.**

Chronic fatigue syndrome makes simple activities difficult. Even getting out of bed is often impossible. Still, I've never allowed my illness to define who I am. I read my Bible every day, even if it means only reading a few verses or having a family member read to me. I owe my family a great deal. Dad even gave up a privilege of responsibility at a convention so that he could help me attend. He never complained. He said the greatest privilege he could have is to take care of his family. **"**

**KATSUTOSHI, 20** **"Suddenly, in a panic, I'll scream and shake violently, even throwing things around and breaking things.**

I've had epilepsy since I was five years old. My attacks have occurred up to seven times a month. I have to take medication each day, and as a result, I tire easily. But I try to think of others, not just myself. In my congregation

there are two full-time ministers my age who have been a big support. When I graduated from school, I increased my share in the ministry. Epilepsy is a daily struggle. But when I feel down, I make sure to get my rest. By the next day, I'm in a better frame of mind. **"**

Why do I have to be so sick? **77**

■ **MATTHEW, 19** ❝It's difficult to gain the respect of your peers when you don't fit their definition of 'normal.'❞

I would love to play sports, but I can't. I have cerebral palsy, and even walking is difficult. Still, I don't dwell on what I can't do. I immerse myself in activities that I can perform, such as reading. The Kingdom Hall is a place where I can be myself without having to worry about being judged. It's also comforting to know that Jehovah loves me for the person I am on the inside. In fact, I really don't view myself as a disabled person. I see myself as a person with an extra and unique challenge to overcome. ❞

■ **MIKI, 25** ❝I used to be able to play sports. Then, while still in my teens, it was as if I suddenly grew old.❞

I was born with atrial septal defect—a hole in the heart. The symptoms became manifest when I was a teenager. I underwent surgery, but now—six years later—I still tire easily and get chronic headaches. So I set attainable, short-term goals for myself. For instance, I have been able to serve as a full-time minister, much of which I accomplish through letter writing and telephone witnessing. Also, my illness has helped me to acquire qualities that I didn't have, such as long-suffering and modesty. ❞

• • • • • • • • •

(*Continued from page 74*)

Bible says: "With evil things God cannot be tried nor does he himself try anyone." (James 1:13) Sickness is merely part of the present human condition, and all of us are subject to "time and unforeseen occurrence."—Ecclesiastes 9:11.

Happily, Jehovah God has promised a new world in which "no resident will say: 'I am sick.' " (Isaiah 33:24) Even those who have died will be resurrected, so that they will have opportunity to enjoy that new world. (John 5:28, 29) In the meantime, though, how can you make the best of your situation?

**Try to be positive.** The Bible says: "A heart that is joyful does good as a curer." (Proverbs 17:22) Some might feel that joy and laughter are inappropriate in the face of serious illness. But good-natured humor and pleasant company can refresh your mind and increase your will to live. So think about what you can do to bring more joy into your life. Remember, joy is a godly quality, part of the fruitage of God's spirit. (Galatians 5:22) That spirit can help you to endure illness with a measure of joy.—Psalm 41:3.

**Set realistic goals.** "Wisdom is with the modest ones," says the Bible. (Proverbs 11:2) Modesty will help you to be neither reckless nor

---

**DID YOU KNOW . . .**

Your illness or disability is not a punishment from God. Rather, it is the result of the imperfection that all of us have inherited from Adam. —Romans 5:12.

---

overprotective. For example, if your condition permits it, appropriate physical activity can help you feel better. That's why medical facilities often have physical therapy programs for young patients. In many cases proper exercise not only promotes physical healing but also helps to keep your spirits up. The point is, honestly assess your situation and set realistic goals.

**Learn to deal with others.** What if some make insensitive remarks about your condition? The Bible says: "Do not give your heart to all the words that people may speak." (Ecclesiastes 7:21) Sometimes the best way to handle such talk is simply to ignore it. Or perhaps you can head off the situation. If, for example, others seem to be tense around you because you're confined to a wheelchair, try putting them at ease. You might say: "You're probably wondering why I have to use a wheelchair. Would you like to know?"

**TIP**

Knowledge reduces fear of the unknown. So learn as much as you can about your condition. Ask your doctor specific questions if you're not clear on some matter.

**Don't give up.** In the face of great suffering, Jesus prayed to God, trusted in Him, and concentrated on his own joyful future rather than on the pain. (Hebrews 12:2) He learned from his hard experiences. (Hebrews 4:15, 16; 5:7-9) He accepted help and encouragement. (Luke 22:43) He focused on the welfare of others rather than on his own discomfort.—Luke 23:39-43; John 19:26, 27.

## Jehovah "Cares for You"

Whatever your difficulty, you need not feel that God views you as damaged. On the contrary, Jehovah sees those who strive to please him as precious and valuable.

**READ MORE ABOUT THIS TOPIC IN VOLUME 1, CHAPTER 13**

(Luke 12:7) "He cares for you" in a very personal way, and he's pleased to use you in his service—despite your illness or disability.—1 Peter 5:7.

So don't allow fear or uncertainty to hold you back from doing the things that you want and need to do. Always look to Jehovah God for support. He understands your needs and your feelings. Furthermore, he can provide you with "the power beyond what is normal" to help you to endure. (2 Corinthians 4:7) In time, perhaps you will have the optimistic viewpoint of Timothy, who was diagnosed with chronic fatigue syndrome at age 17. He says: "According to 1 Corinthians 10:13, Jehovah won't let us go through more

### ▶▶▶ action plan!

*To keep a positive outlook despite my illness or disability, I will*

✎ .........................................................................................................

.........................................................................................................

*One realistic goal I can set is*

.........................................................................................................

*If someone says unkind things to me about my condition, I will put the matter in perspective by*

.........................................................................................................

.........................................................................................................

*What I would like to ask my parent(s) about this subject is*

.........................................................................................................

.........................................................................................................

than we can bear. I reason that if my Creator is confident that I can cope with this trial, who am I to argue?"

## If Someone You Know Is Sick

What if you're healthy, but you know someone who is sick or disabled? How can you help that one? The key is to show "fellow feeling" and to be "tenderly compassionate." (1 Peter 3:8) Try to understand what that person is going through. See his challenges through *his* eyes rather than your own. Nina, who was born with spina bifida, says: "Since my body is small and I'm in a wheelchair, some people talk to me as if I were a child, which can be discouraging to me. Others, though, make an effort to *sit down* and talk to me, so that we're at the same eye level. I really enjoy that!"

If you look beyond their infirmities, you'll discover that those who have health challenges are a lot like you. And think of it—by your words you have the power to 'impart a spiritual gift' to such ones! When you do so, you too will experience a blessing, for there will be "an interchange of encouragement."—Romans 1:11, 12.

---

**WHAT DO YOU THINK?**

- How can you use the information in this chapter to help someone who's disabled or chronically ill?

- If you have a chronic illness, what positive things can you meditate on to make the best of your condition?

- How do you know that affliction isn't a sign of God's disapproval?

---

*Describe the one thing you dislike most about yourself and explain why it bothers you.*

*Write down one thing you like about yourself and describe why you feel this is an asset.*

# FRIENDSHIP ISSUES 3

*How important is it to you to have friends?*
- ❏ Not important
- ❏ Somewhat important
- ❏ Very important

*Do you find it easy to make friends?*
- ❏ Yes
- ❏ No

*Do you have a best friend?*
- ❏ Yes
- ❏ No

*What one quality would you most expect of a friend?*

..................................................

The Bible says that "a true companion is loving all the time, and is a brother that is born for when there is distress." (Proverbs 17:17) That's the kind of companion *you* need! But making friends can be difficult, and keeping them can be even harder. How can you create and maintain the best kind of friendships? Consider the advice presented in **Chapters 9-12.**

# How can I deal with loneliness?

*It's a beautiful day, and you have no plans. All your friends do, though. They're out having a good time. Once again, you've been left out! Being among the uninvited is bad enough, but what it implies is even worse. 'Maybe there's something wrong with me,' you say to yourself. 'Why doesn't anyone want my company?'*

*You can bridge the chasm that separates you from your peers*

PERHAPS, more than once, you've been in the situation described on the opposite page. You may feel as if a wide chasm separates you from your peers. You stammer every time you try to start a conversation with them. When you *do* have an opportunity to socialize, shyness rears its head. Why is simple socializing so difficult?

Rather than remain stuck on your side of the chasm, you can build some bridges. Let's see how.

● **Chasm 1: A negative view of yourself.** Some youths relentlessly put themselves down. They're convinced that no one likes them and that they have nothing worthwhile to add to a conversation. Is that the way you feel about yourself? If so, a negative self-image will only widen the chasm that separates you from your peers.

**The bridge: Focus on your assets.** (2 Corinthians 11:6) Ask yourself, 'What are my strengths?' Think of some talents or positive qualities that you possess and list them below. ✎ ....................................................................

....................................................................................

....................................................................................

> **One Christian sister was reaching out to me, but for a time I didn't respond to her. When I finally did, I felt so foolish! She's turned out to be one of the best friends I've ever had, even though she's 25 years older than I am!** —Marie

No doubt you have flaws, and it's good to be aware of these. (1 Corinthians 10:12) But you also have much to offer. Recognizing your assets will give you the confidence you need to break free from a negative self-image.

● **Chasm 2: Shyness.** You'd love to start a conversation, but when the opportunity arises, you just can't seem to open your mouth. "I'm in a permanent state of shyness," laments 19-year-old Elizabeth. "I find it extremely hard to approach people at Christian meetings, and I really admire those who can do it!" If you're like Elizabeth, you may feel as if this chasm is impossible to cross.

**The bridge: Take a genuine interest in others.** Don't worry—you don't have to turn into an extrovert. Start by showing interest in just one person. "Simply asking others how they are doing or asking them about their work helps you to get to know them better," says a youth named Jorge.

Here's a tip: Don't limit yourself to people of your own age. Some of the warmest friendships recorded in the Bible were between people with considerable age differ-

**? DID YOU KNOW . . .**

**The Bible indicates that Moses, Jeremiah, and Timothy may have had a problem with shyness.—Exodus 3:11, 13; 4:1, 10; Jeremiah 1:6-8; 1 Timothy 4:12; 2 Timothy 1:6-8.**

**READ MORE ABOUT THIS TOPIC IN VOLUME 1, CHAPTERS 8 AND 14**

ences, such as Ruth and Naomi, David and Jonathan, and Timothy and Paul. (Ruth 1:16, 17; 1 Samuel 18:1; 1 Corinthians 4:17) Remember, too, that conversation is an interchange, not a solo performance. People appreciate good listeners. So if you tend to be shy, remember—you don't have to carry the whole conversation!

Write down the names of two adults you would like to get to know better. ✎ ................................................................
................................................................................................

Why not approach one of the people you listed above and strike up a conversation? The more you reach out to "the whole association of brothers," the less lonely you'll feel.—1 Peter 2:17.

● **Chasm 3: Disagreeable behavior.** The know-it-all is always ready with an insult, a wisecrack, or a put-down. Then there's the person who just loves to argue and force his opinions on everyone. Being "righteous overmuch," he quickly condemns anyone who doesn't live up to his personal standards. (Ecclesiastes 7:16) In all likelihood, you can't stand being around people like that! Could it be, though, that a chasm has formed because *you* act that way? The Bible says: "The foolish one speaks many words," and also "in the abundance of words there does not fail to be transgression."—Ecclesiastes 10:14; Proverbs 10:19.

**The bridge: Cultivate "fellow feeling."** (1 Peter 3:8) Even if you don't agree with another's view, patiently allow

> **TIP** ✔
>
> **Keep conversation moving forward. For example, if someone asks if you enjoyed the weekend, don't just say yes. Explain *why* you enjoyed it. Then ask how the other person passed the time.**

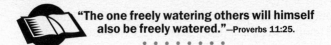

**"The one freely watering others will himself also be freely watered."**—Proverbs 11:25.

• • • • • • • •

that one to talk. Dwell on points that you agree on. If you feel you must express disagreement on some issue, do so in a mild and tactful way.

Speak to others the way you would want to be spoken to. The Bible's advice is to "keep doing all things free from murmurings and arguments." (Philippians 2:14) Needless bickering or teasing, as well as insulting others or self-righteously condemning them, simply alienates people. They will like you a lot more if you "let your utterance be always with graciousness."—Colossians 4:6.

### At All Costs?

After this brief self-examination, perhaps you see some ways that you can build bridges to cross the chasm that may have developed between you and others. Of

## >>> action plan!

*The chasm I encounter most is*

..................................................................................................

..................................................................................................

*I will work to build a bridge in this area by*

..................................................................................................

..................................................................................................

*What I would like to ask my parent(s) about this subject is*

..................................................................................................

..................................................................................................

course, you have to be realistic. You can't expect *everyone* to like you. Jesus said that some would even hate those who do what is right. (John 15:19) So it doesn't pay to try to win friends at all costs.

Nevertheless, while not compromising your Bible-based standards, you can make reasonable efforts to be pleasant and agreeable. Samuel of Bible times was firmly resolved to do what would please God. The result? He kept growing "more likable both from Jehovah's standpoint and from that of men." (1 Samuel 2:26) With a little effort, so will you!

**IN OUR NEXT CHAPTER** *Your best friend is suddenly acting like your worst enemy. What can you do about it?*

## WHAT DO YOU THINK?

- Why might some Christians be lonely?

- What can help you to look at yourself in a balanced way, instead of being consumed by negative thoughts?

- How would you comfort a younger brother or sister who is battling loneliness?

# 10

# Why did my friend hurt me?

*"Kerry was my very good friend. I picked her up after work each day, since she didn't have a car. Soon, though, I began to feel that she was taking advantage of me.*

*"She would get into the car busily talking or text-messaging on her cell phone. She never said thank you for the rides, and she stopped contributing for gas. And her conversation was negative. I became furious with myself for putting up with her for so long!*

*"One day I kindly explained to Kerry that I wouldn't be able to pick her up after work anymore. Since then, she hasn't sought out my company—which convinces me all the more that she only valued my friendship for what she could get out of me. And it really hurts!"*
—*Nicole.*

IT CAN happen to the best of friends. One day the two are inseparable; the next day they aren't even talking to each other. How does a sweet friendship turn sour so fast?

● For Jeremy, everything seemed to change when a good friend moved about a thousand miles away. "After he moved, he never called," Jeremy says, "and that really hurt me."

● Kerrin started noticing a personality change in her best friend of five years. "Her attitude and speech really worried me," Kerrin says. "She became negative and cynical about things that were important to me. When we tried to talk it out, she accused me of being self-righteous and disloyal and said that our friendship wasn't healthy for her!"

● For Gloria, the end of a close friendship came without warning or explanation. "At first, we hit it off great," Gloria says, "and she told me that I was like a sister to her. Then, out of nowhere, she stopped doing things with me, and she'd make up really lame excuses."

● The trouble between Laura and Daria began when Daria stole Laura's boyfriend. "She would talk with him on the phone for hours, even though he and I were dating," Laura says. "I was betrayed by my best friend and lost a potential marriage mate—both at the same time!"

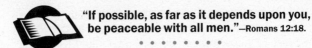

**"If possible, as far as it depends upon you, be peaceable with all men."**—Romans 12:18.

• • • • • • • •

## What Went Wrong?

Everyone makes mistakes. So it's only to be expected that sooner or later a friend will do or say something that hurts you. To be honest, you may recall a few times when you have hurt others. (Ecclesiastes 7:22) "We're all imperfect, and we're going to rub one another the wrong way once in a while," says a girl named Lisa. Usually a rift that's caused by a minor misunderstanding can be cleared up with a brief conversation.

In other cases, though, a rift in a friendship isn't the result of a single event but is caused by a gradual realization that the two of you aren't as similar as you once thought. Remember, as you grow, your interests change—and so do those of your friend. What can you do when you sense that you and a friend are drifting apart?

## How to Mend a Friendship

Have you ever torn one of your favorite articles of clothing? What did you do? Throw it away? or repair it? No doubt, much depended on the extent of the damage and how much you

*A rift in a friendship is like a tear in a garment—but both can be mended*

> **If I had it all to do again, I would not have expected perfection from our friendship. I would have listened more and supported him and not magnified his flaws. I understand now that what makes a successful friendship is working through the tests and challenges.** —Keenon

valued the garment. If you really loved that article of clothing, you probably looked for ways to repair it. In many cases, the same is possible with a damaged friendship. Much depends on what has happened and how much you value the relationship.*

For instance, if you've been the victim of some unkind word or deed, you may be able to cover over the problem by following the advice of Psalm 4:4: "Have your say in your heart, upon your bed, and keep silent." So before throwing away the friendship, think carefully. Was the act intentional? If you can't be sure, why not give your friend the benefit of the doubt? In many cases you can let 'love cover a multitude of sins.'—1 Peter 4:8.

You might also examine whether you contributed to the problem. For example, if a friend betrays a confidence, could it be that it was unwise on your part to burden your friend with the information in

---

* Some companions may not be worth keeping as close associates. This would especially be true if their conduct is no longer appropriate for a Christian.—1 Corinthians 5:11; 15:33.

---

**DID YOU KNOW...**

People in healthy relationships give each other a measure of space. (Proverbs 25:17) In contrast, becoming overly possessive of a friend's time and attention can smother a relationship.

READ MORE ABOUT THIS TOPIC IN VOLUME 1, CHAPTER 8

Why did my friend hurt me?

the first place? Another question you could consider is whether you set yourself up as a target for ridicule—perhaps by excessive or foolish talking. (Proverbs 15:2) If so, ask yourself, 'Do I need to make changes so that my friend will respect me more?'

## "Can We Talk About What Happened?"

What, though, if you feel that you cannot simply dismiss the matter? In that case it might be best to approach your friend. But be careful not to do so when you're angry. The Bible states: "An enraged man stirs up contention, but one that is slow to anger quiets down quarreling." (Proverbs 15:18) So wait until you've cooled down before you attempt to resolve the situation.

When you *do* approach your friend, remember that your objective isn't to "return evil for evil." (Romans 12:17) Rather, your goal is to settle matters and restore

### >>> action plan!

*If I need to approach a friend about a hurt that he or she has caused, I could start by saying*

✎ ......................................................................................

......................................................................................

*Even when upset at what a friend has done, I will seek to maintain peace by*

......................................................................................

......................................................................................

*What I would like to ask my parent(s) about this subject is*

......................................................................................

......................................................................................

**ROLE MODEL**

# Lydia

Although she is a new believer, Lydia **takes the initiative** to show hospitality to Paul and his companions. (Acts 16:14, 15) As a result, she has the privilege of enjoying the company of these disciples. After Paul and Silas are released from prison, where do they go? Right back to the home of Lydia!—Acts 16:40.

Like Lydia, can you take the initiative to get to know others? How can you do so? **Start small.** Work on talking to one person at a time. You could make it a goal to **start a conversation** with one person each time you attend a Christian meeting. Try to smile. If you don't know what to say, **ask questions** or share something about yourself. Be a **good listener.** In time, you may be inclined to say more. People often respond to sincere words that are kind and pleasant. (Proverbs 16:24) Because of her friendly and hospitable nature, Lydia was blessed with **good friends.** If you imitate her example, you will be too!

**TIP**

Before jumping to conclusions, get your friend's side of the story.—Proverbs 18:13.

the friendship. (Psalm 34:14) So speak from the heart. You could say, "We've been friends for some time. Can we talk about what happened?" Once you know the cause of the problem, it may be easier to mend the friendship. Even if your friend is unresponsive, you can find comfort in the fact that *you* have tried to restore peace.

In the end, be assured that although "there exist companions disposed to break one another to pieces," there's also "a friend sticking closer than a brother." (Proverbs 18:24) Granted, even the best of friendships may undergo occasional strain. When that happens, do whatever you can to mend the relationship. Really, being willing to patch up differences is evidence that you're becoming a mature adult.

**IN OUR NEXT CHAPTER** *Some of your peers may spend hours chatting on the Internet. What's the attraction?*

---

**WHAT DO YOU THINK?**

- Why do friends sometimes drift apart?

- What type of offenses might you be able to resolve in your heart, and what type of offenses would you need to talk over with the friend who hurt you?

- What beneficial lessons can you learn from going through the experience of being hurt by a friend?

- What precautions can you take in order to reduce the chances of being hurt by a friend?

# 11

# What about online friendships?

| | |
|---|---|
| ***Which form of communication do you prefer?*** | ❏ Face-to-face<br>❏ Phone<br>❏ Computer |
| ***Whom do you find it easiest to converse with?*** | ❏ Classmates<br>❏ Family members<br>❏ Fellow Christians |
| ***Where does your communication tend to be least inhibited?*** | ❏ At school<br>❏ At home<br>❏ At congregation meetings |

LOOK at your answer to the first question. Did you indicate that you prefer to communicate by computer rather than talk face-to-face? If so, you're far from being alone. Many youths use the Internet to start and maintain friendships. "The idea of being able to meet people from around the world—people you'd never be able to meet otherwise—is alluring," says a young woman named Elaine. Tammy, 19, points out another enticement. "You can control how people view you," she says. "When you're face-to-face, if you don't fit in, there's nothing you can do about it."

Now look at your answers to the second and third questions. Don't be surprised if you find it easier to converse with classmates than with fellow Christians at congregation meetings. "At school, there's a greater chance of finding people who are going through the same things you are," says 18-year-old Jasmine. "That can make them a lot easier to warm up to."

Put all the above factors together, and it may seem only natural that you would want to chat with schoolmates online. Tammy admits that for a time she did that. "All my schoolmates talked online about things, and I didn't want to be left out," she says.* Natalie, 20, set up a Web page to keep in touch with friends. "Technology is advancing," she says. "Communication is finding new forms. This is one of them, and I like it."

## Weighing the Dangers

There's no question that, for some, making and maintaining friendships is easier online. "The Internet gives you a form of confidence that you wouldn't otherwise have," says Natalie. Tammy would agree. "If you're shy," she says, "communicating online gives you a chance to plan exactly what you will say."

But there are dangers to communicating online, and it would be foolish for you to ignore them. To illustrate: Would you walk blindfolded through the streets of a dangerous neighborhood? Why, then, wander online without being aware of the dangers?

**? DID YOU KNOW...**

It only takes a few online details—perhaps your last name, the name of your school, and your phone number—to enable someone with bad intentions to find you.

Consider the dangers of trying to find friends over the Internet. "It's too easy to meet shady people," says Elaine, who at one time enjoyed casually chatting with strangers online. She adds: "Sometimes it's only a matter

* School friendships will be discussed further in Chapter 17.

of minutes before someone makes lewd remarks or asks such questions as: 'Are you a virgin? Do you do oral sex?' Some even offer cybersex."

What if you're just chatting with a trusted friend? Even then, you need to be careful. "You could spend too much time conversing with someone of the opposite sex, even if that person is 'just a friend,'" says Joan. "The more time you spend sending messages to that person, the closer your friendship becomes, and conversation has the potential of becoming much more intimate."

### "Those Who Hide What They Are"

King David well knew the value of guarding against the wrong kind of friends. He wrote: "I have not sat with men of untruth; and with those who hide what they are I do not come in."—Psalm 26:4.

While online, have you encountered the type of people David spoke of? Under what circumstances do people online "hide what they are"? ✎ ...............................................

.......................................................................................

On the other hand, could it be that *you* hide what you are while online? "I would start conversations with people

*Would you walk blindfolded through the streets of a dangerous neighborhood? Then why communicate online without being alert to the dangers?*

**"I have not sat with men of untruth; and with those who hide what they are I do not come in."**—Psalm 26:4.

• • • • • • • • •

and then take on a personality to fit the conversation," says Abigail, who visited chat rooms.

A girl named Leanne employed another form of deception. She relates: "I regularly communicated online with a boy in a neighboring congregation. We were soon voicing our feelings of 'love.' I would minimize the page on the screen when my parents walked by, so they never had a clue as to what was going on. I don't think they thought it possible that their 13-year-old daughter was writing love poems to a 14-year-old boy. It never entered their heads."

> ✓ **TIP**
>
> Time flies when you're on the Internet! So set a time limit and stick to it. If need be, set an alarm to go off when your scheduled time is up.

### Staying Safe

Of course, there are times when online communication is appropriate. For example, many people—adults included—use the Internet to keep in touch with friends. If that's true of you, are there any precautions you can take? Consider the following points.

● **Monitor the amount of time you spend online,** and don't let it rob you of time for more important things—including sleep. "Some kids at school said they stayed up till three in the morning on the Internet," says a youth named Brian.—Ephesians 5:15, 16.

● **Communicate only with people you know or whose identity you can verify.** Unsavory individuals regularly

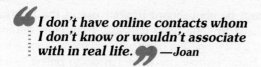

> **I don't have online contacts whom I don't know or wouldn't associate with in real life.** —*Joan*

troll the Internet looking to exploit unsuspecting youths. —Romans 16:18.

● **When conducting a business transaction, be cautious.** Be extremely careful about giving out personal information. Otherwise, you could become a victim of fraud —or worse.—Matthew 10:16.

● **When sending photos to your friends, ask yourself,** 'Does this truly represent someone who claims to serve God?'—Titus 2:7, 8.

● **As with face-to-face communication,** if an online discussion turns toward "things which are not becoming," end the conversation.—Ephesians 5:3, 4.

## ⟫⟫ *action plan!*

*I would like to limit my time on the Internet to ........................
per week, and to do this I will*

✎ ...........................................................................................................

............................................................................................................

............................................................................................................

*If I find myself talking to a stranger on the Internet,
I will*

............................................................................................................

............................................................................................................

*What I would like to ask my parent(s) about this
subject is*

............................................................................................................

............................................................................................................

● **Always be aboveboard in your use of the Internet.** If you have to 'hide what you are' from your parents, something's wrong. "I'm open with my mom," says a teen named Kari. "I show her what I'm doing online."—Hebrews 13:18.

## "It's Worth the Wait!"

You want friends. That's normal. Humans were created to enjoy the company of others. (Genesis 2:18) So when you feel the urge to have friends, *that's in harmony with the way you were made!* Just be careful how you choose them.

Be assured that you can find the best of friends if you choose them according to the standards of God's Word. One 15-year-old girl put it this way: "It's hard to find friends who love Jehovah and love you. But when you do find them, it's worth the wait!"

**IN OUR NEXT CHAPTER** *Who said words can't hurt? Gossip can stab like a sword. How can you put a stop to it?*

---

**WHAT DO YOU THINK?**

- What are the pros and cons of online communication compared with face-to-face conversation?

- Why is it easy to adopt a different personality when conversing online?

- How can you control the amount of time you spend online?

- In what beneficial ways might Internet communication be used?

**12**

# What's so bad about gossip?

*"Once I went to a party, and the next day rumors were spread that I had had sex with one of the boys there. That wasn't true at all!"*—Linda.

*"Sometimes I'll hear a rumor that I'm dating someone—someone whom, in fact, I don't even know! Many people who gossip don't bother to check the facts."*—Mike.

GOSSIP can fill your life with more intrigue than a feature film. Just ask 19-year-old Amber. "I've been a *constant* victim," she says. "It was rumored that I was pregnant, that I'd had abortions, and that I was selling drugs, buying drugs, and doing drugs. Why would people say these things about me? Really, I have no idea!"

Armed with e-mail and instant messaging, a boy or a girl with malicious intent can tarnish your reputation without even speaking a word. All it takes is a few keystrokes to send a vicious rumor on its way to dozens of eager recipients! In some cases an entire Web site has been set up just to humiliate someone. More commonly, online blogs are glutted with gossip that would never be uttered in person.

But is talking about others *always* bad? Could there be such a thing as . . .

### *Good* Gossip?

Mark the following statement true or false.

***Gossip is always bad.*** ✎❏ True ❏ False

What's the correct response? Really, it depends on how you define "gossip." If the word merely means casual talk, there may be times when it's appropriate. After all, the Bible tells us to "be interested in the lives of others." (Philippians 2:4, *New Century Version*) Not that we should meddle in matters that don't concern us. (1 Peter 4: 15) But informal conversation often provides useful information, such as who's getting

> **I really learned my lesson when the person I gossiped about found out and confronted me. There was no way to sidestep the issue! I definitely learned that it's better to be up front with someone than to be talking behind that person's back!** —Paula

married or who had a baby. Let's face it—we can't say we care about others if we never talk about them!

Still, casual talk can easily turn into harmful gossip. For example, the innocent remark "Bob and Sue would make a good couple" might be repeated as "Bob and Sue *are* a couple"—even though Bob and Sue know nothing of their supposed romance. 'Not a serious problem,' you might say—unless, of course, you were Bob or Sue!

Julie, 18, was the victim of that kind of gossip, and it hurt. "It made me angry," she says, "and it raised doubts in my mind about trusting others." Jane, 19, was in a similar situation. "I ended up avoiding the boy I was supposedly dating," she says, adding, "It didn't seem fair, as we were friends, and I felt that we should be able to talk without rumors starting!"

### Steer Your Conversations Carefully

How can you control your tongue when tempted to gossip? To answer that question, think of the skill that's required to drive on a busy highway. Unexpectedly, a situation may arise that makes it necessary for you to change lanes, yield, or come to a complete stop. If you're alert, you see what's ahead and react accordingly.

It's similar with conversation. You can usually tell when a discussion is veering into harmful gossip. When

*Harmful gossip is like a dangerous weapon that can destroy another's reputation*

that happens, can you skillfully 'change lanes'? If you don't, be forewarned—gossip can do damage. "I said something unkind about a girl—that she was boy crazy—and it got back to her," relates Mike. "I'll never forget her voice when she confronted me, how hurt she was over my thoughtless remark. We smoothed things over, but I didn't feel good knowing that I had hurt someone in that way!"

There's no doubt that words can hurt. Even the Bible acknowledges that "there exists the one speaking thoughtlessly as with the stabs of a sword." (Proverbs 12: 18) That's all the more reason to weigh your words before speaking! True, it may take self-control to put the brakes on a juicy discussion. Still, it's as 17-year-old Carolyn points out: "You need to be careful of what you say. If you haven't heard it from a reliable source, you could be spreading lies." So when it comes to potentially harmful gossip, apply the apostle Paul's advice to

> **TIP**
>
> If you hear gossip, you could respond by saying: "I don't feel comfortable talking about this. After all, she's not here to defend herself."

"make it your aim to live quietly and to mind your own business."—1 Thessalonians 4:11.

How can you show personal interest in others and still mind your own business? Before talking about someone, ask yourself: 'Do I really know the facts? What's my motive in relating this information? How will my gossiping affect *my* reputation?' That last question is important, for being known as a gossip says more about *your* character than that of the person being talked about.

## When *You* Are the Victim

What can you do if you're the victim of gossip? "Do not hurry yourself in your spirit to become offended," warns Ecclesiastes 7:9. Instead, try to put the matter in perspective. The Bible says: "Do not give your heart to all the words that people may speak, . . . for your own heart well knows even many times that you, even you, have called down evil upon others."—Ecclesiastes 7:21, 22.

### ▶▶▶ action plan!

*The next time I'm tempted to spread a rumor, I will*

✎ ........................................................................

........................................................................

*If unkind things have been said about me,
I will deal with the situation by*

........................................................................

........................................................................

*What I would like to ask my parent(s) about this
subject is*

........................................................................

........................................................................

**"The one guarding his mouth is keeping his soul. The one opening wide his lips —he will have ruin."**—Proverbs 13:3.

• • • • • • • •

Of course, there's no excuse for harmful gossip. Yet, overreacting may cast a more negative light on you than the actual gossip! Why not, then, adopt the view that helped Renee? "I'm usually hurt when someone says something bad about me, but I try to keep it in perspective," she says. "I mean, next week they'll probably be talking about someone or something else."*

Have the good sense, then, to steer conversations away from harmful gossip. And when unkind talk involves you, have the maturity not to overreact. Let your good works speak for you. (1 Peter 2:12) If you do, you will help to preserve a good relationship with others and to maintain a good standing with God.

---

* In some circumstances, it may be wise to find a tactful way to confront the gossiper. In many cases, though, this isn't even necessary, as "love covers a multitude of sins."—1 Peter 4:8.

**WHAT DO YOU THINK?**

- **When would it be appropriate to talk about the interests of others?**

- **Have you ever been the victim of gossip, and if so, what did you learn from the experience?**

- **How can spreading gossip about others damage *your* reputation?**

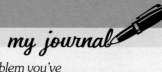

*my journal*

*Describe a recent friendship problem you've experienced.*

✎

_____

_____

_____

_____

_____

*In the light of what you've read in this section, how might you choose to handle this problem?*

_____

_____

_____

_____

_____

_____

_____

# 4 SCHOOL AND YOUR PEERS

**Do you struggle just to keep a passing grade in certain subjects?**
- ☐ Yes
- ☐ No

**Have you ever been bullied or sexually harassed at school?**
- ☐ Yes
- ☐ No

**Are you sometimes tempted to join your peers in improper conduct?**
- ☐ Yes
- ☐ No

'If I can make it through school, I can survive *any-thing!'* you might say to yourself. And there's an element of truth in that statement. After all, school is a testing ground for your mental, emotional, and spiritual fiber. How can you obtain a well-rounded education without being contaminated by the ungodly attitudes of some of your peers? **Chapters 13-17** will help you acquire the skills you need.

**13**

# How can I do better at school?

IMAGINE that you're trapped in a dense, dark jungle. Virtually all sunlight is blocked by the lush canopy overhead. Surrounded by thick vegetation, you can barely move. To escape, you must cut your way through with a machete.

Some would say that the experience of school is similar to the scene described above. After all, you're trapped all day in the classroom and hemmed in at night by hours of homework. Is that how you feel? On the line below, write down which school subject you find *most* challenging.

✎ ......................................................................................................

Perhaps your parents and teachers have urged you to put forth more effort in this subject. If so, they're not trying to make your life difficult! They just want you to reach your full potential. So, what can you do if the pressure to measure up makes you want to give up? With the proper tools, you can clear a path through the jungle. What are these tools?

● **Tool 1: A healthy attitude toward learning.** It's hard to be motivated to do well in school if you have a negative view of learning. So try to see the big picture. The Christian apostle Paul wrote: "The man who plows ought to plow in hope and the man who threshes ought to do so in hope of being a partaker." —1 Corinthians 9:10.

Seeing the value of "plowing" through certain subjects may not be easy. Why? Because not everything in your curriculum may seem relevant—at least not now. Still,

| DID YOU KNOW... ❓ |
| :--- |
| Cheating can lead to loss of trust as well as stunted academic growth. Above all, it harms your relationship with God.—Proverbs 11:1. |

*Getting through school can be like cutting your way through a dense jungle—but both are possible with the right tools*

an education in a variety of subjects will enrich your understanding of the world around you. It will help you to "become all things to people of all sorts," giving you the ability to talk to people of various backgrounds. (1 Corinthians 9: 22) At the very least, you will improve your thinking ability—a skill that will surely help you in the long run.

● **Tool 2: A positive view of your abilities.** School can reveal your hidden talents. Paul wrote to Timothy: "Stir up like a fire the gift of God which is in you." (2 Timothy 1:6) Evidently, Timothy had been appointed to some special service in the Christian congregation. But his God-given ability—his "gift"—needed to be cultivated so that it would not lie dormant or go to waste. Of course, your scholastic abilities are not directly bestowed upon you by God. Nevertheless, the talents you have are unique to you. School can help you to discover and nurture abilities that you never knew you had.

Don't set yourself up for disaster by thinking that you're simply not capable of improving. When beset with

READ MORE ABOUT THIS TOPIC IN VOLUME 1, CHAPTER 18

> *I see it in other youths my age. The study habits they had in school carried over to their personal study habits in spiritual matters. Those who didn't learn to like studying in school weren't that interested in personal Bible study either.* — Sylvie

negative thoughts about your abilities, replace them with positive thoughts. For example, when people, perhaps unjustifiably, criticized Paul's speaking ability, he replied: "Even if I am unskilled in speech, I certainly am not in knowledge." (2 Corinthians 10:10; 11:6) Paul was aware of his weaknesses. But he also knew his strengths.

What about you? What are your strengths? If you cannot think of them, why not ask a supportive adult? Such a friend can help you to identify your strengths and to make the most of them.

● **Tool 3: Good study habits.** There's no shortcut to success at school. Sooner or later, you have to *study*. Granted, that very word might have an unpleasant ring to it. However, study is beneficial. In fact, with a little effort, you may find it enjoyable.

To cultivate good study habits, though, you will need to organize your time. Remember—while you're in school, study should be a

---

**TIP** ✔

When studying, first *survey* the material, getting an overview of it. Next, make up *questions* based on main headings. Then *read* the material, looking for the answers. Finally, see if you can *recall* what you've read.

**"He that is watching the wind will not sow seed; and he that is looking at the clouds will not reap."**—Ecclesiastes 11:4.

• • • • • • • • •

priority. True, the Bible says that there's "a time to laugh" and "a time to skip about." (Ecclesiastes 3:1, 4; 11:9) So, like most youths, you probably want to leave some time for recreation.* But Ecclesiastes 11:4 warns: "He that is watching the wind will not sow seed; and he that is looking at the clouds will not reap." The lesson? Study first, play second. Don't worry—you *can* find time for both!

## Help for Your Homework

What, though, if you're simply swamped with homework? Perhaps you feel as did 17-year-old Sandrine, who said: "I spend from two to three hours a night on my

---

* For more information on recreation, see Section 8 of this book.

>>> *action plan!*

*On my next report card, I would like ____ to be my grade in
the following subject:*

✎ ......................................................................................................

*I will strive to improve in that subject by doing the
following:*

......................................................................................................

......................................................................................................

*What I would like to ask my parent(s) about this
subject is*

......................................................................................................

......................................................................................................

**Find a study area.** It should be free of distractions. Use a desk if possible. Don't have the TV on.

**Set priorities.** Since your schooling is important, resolve that you won't turn on the TV until your homework is done.

**Don't procrastinate.** Have a definite schedule for your homework, and stick to it.

**Have a plan.** Decide which project you should tackle first, which one second, and so forth. List these on paper, and give each one a time limit. Cross off each assignment as you complete it.

**Take breaks.** If you find yourself losing focus, stop for a brief rest. But get back to your homework as soon as possible.

**Have confidence in yourself.** Remember, the difference between a good student and a poor one usually has more to do with diligence than intelligence. You *can* make a success of school. Put forth the effort, and you will reap the rewards.

homework, plus the weekends." How can you cope with the onslaught? Try the suggestions on page 119.

## Clearing the Path

Regarding matters pertaining to spiritual progress, Paul wrote to Timothy: "Give your whole attention, all your energies, to these things, so that your progress is plain for all to see." (1 Timothy 4:15, *Phillips*) Similarly, with diligent effort, your academic progress will be evident.

Think of the illustration presented at the outset of this chapter. Trapped in a dense jungle, you would need the proper tool—a machete—to clear a path. The same is true with school. Rather than feel overwhelmed by the demands of your parents and teachers, use the three tools that have been discussed in this chapter to make a success of school. As your performance improves, you'll be glad you did!

**IN OUR NEXT CHAPTER** *As if you didn't have enough problems at school, now you're being harassed. What can you do about it?*

### WHAT DO YOU THINK?

- Why should you apply yourself to your studies at school?

- What kind of study/homework schedule will work for you?

- In your home, where is the best place for you to do your homework and to study?

- How can you keep hobbies and recreation from interfering with your grades?

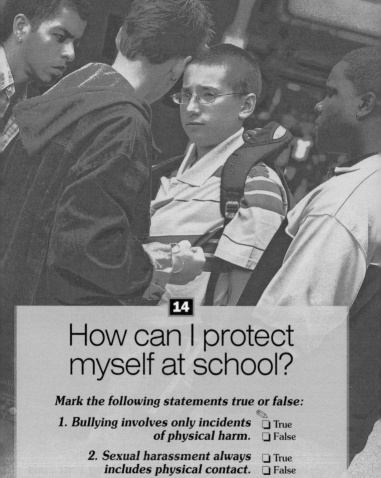

# 14

# How can I protect myself at school?

*Mark the following statements true or false:*

1. Bullying involves only incidents of physical harm.
   ☐ True
   ☐ False

2. Sexual harassment always includes physical contact.
   ☐ True
   ☐ False

3. Girls can bully and harass too.
   ☐ True
   ☐ False

4. If you're being bullied or sexually harassed, there's nothing you can do about it.
   ☐ True
   ☐ False

TERROR is a daily experience for millions of youths who are bullied at school. "The 15-minute bus ride became a torture that seemed to last for hours as my tormentors progressed from verbal abuse to physical mistreatment," says a youth named Ryan. Other youths are sexually harassed. "A very popular boy cornered me in the hallway and started touching me inappropriately," says young Anita. "Asking him in a nice way to keep his hands to himself didn't work. He didn't think I really meant it."

Some teens are even hounded online by their classmates. Are you a victim of mistreatment? If so, what can you do about your plight? Plenty! But first, let's separate the myths from the facts by examining the statements made at the outset of this chapter.

**1. False.** Most bullies use their mouths, not their fists. Threats, insults, sarcasm, and ridicule can be forms of bullying.

**2. False.** Even a "compliment" with sexual overtones, an obscene joke, or ogling can constitute sexual harassment.

**3. True.** Those who bully and harass can be of either gender.

**4. False.** You *can* take measures to stop the mistreatment. Let's see how.

### How to Beat a Bully —Without Using Your Fists

Some bullies want to provoke you just to see how you'll react. But the Bible gives this wise advice: "Do not hurry

**? DID YOU KNOW...**

Wearing certain gang colors or trademarks can single you out for attack. A former gang member says: "If someone dressed like one of us and he was not one of us, most likely he would be a target. Either he would have to join our gang or get himself hurt."

**READ MORE ABOUT THIS TOPIC IN VOLUME 1, CHAPTER 19**

> **If you know there's going to be a fight, you have to mind your own business and go home. Some hang around, and that's when they get into trouble.** —Jairo

yourself in your spirit to become offended." (Ecclesiastes 7:9) The fact is, 'returning evil for evil' could add fuel to the fire and lead to further problems. (Romans 12:17) How, then, can you beat a bully *without* using your fists?

**Take a lighthearted approach.** If a taunt is simply an attempt at humor, try to laugh it off instead of getting offended. "Sometimes it's just a matter of not taking aggressive statements so seriously," says a boy named Eliu. If a bully sees that his words have little effect, he may stop the harassment.

**Use mildness.** The Bible says: "An answer, when mild, turns away rage." (Proverbs 15:1) A kind reply is what the bully least expects, and it can defuse a tense situation. True, keeping coolheaded when under attack takes self-control. But it's always the better course. Proverbs 29:11 says: "All his spirit is what a stupid one lets out, but he that is wise keeps it calm to the last." Mildness is a sign of strength. The mild person isn't easily thrown off balance, while the bully is often insecure, frustrated, or even desperate. For good reason, the Bible states: "He that is

| TIP | ✔ |
| --- | --- |

If you're the target of bullying, be assertive, but not aggressive. Firmly tell the bully to stop. Calmly leave. If the bullying continues, report it.

slow to anger is better than a mighty man."—Proverbs 16:32.

**Protect yourself.** If a situation seems out of control, you may need to find an 'escape route.' Proverbs 17:14 says: "Before the quarrel has burst forth, take your leave." So if violence appears imminent, walk or run away. If escape is impossible, you may need to ward off violence the best way you can.

**Report it.** Your parents have a right to know about what's happening. They can also give you practical advice. For example, they might suggest that you speak to a school official, such as a guidance counselor, about the matter. Be assured that parents and school officials can handle the matter discreetly, so as not to get you into further trouble.

The bottom line? A bully can't win if you refuse to play his game. So don't get sucked into the flames of his anger. Instead, take control of the situation by employing the foregoing suggestions.

*Responding in anger to a bully's taunts is like throwing fuel on a fire*

# how to prevent sexual harassment

**Don't flirt.** It's an open invitation to harassment. The Bible asks: "Can you carry fire against your chest without burning your clothes?" (Proverbs 6:27, *Today's English Version*) The fact is, flirting is playing with fire.

**Watch your association.** It will be assumed that your values match those of your friends. A young girl named Carla says, "If you hang around with ones who give in to the remarks or who enjoy the attention, then you will get harassed too."—1 Corinthians 15:33.

**Be careful how you dress.** Immodest clothing sends out a clear signal that you crave the interest of the opposite sex—and you'll get it.—Galatians 6:7.

**Don't hide your Christian identity.** If you do, no one will have reason to expect you to live up to Christian standards.—Matthew 5:15, 16.

## Coping With Sexual Harassment

If you're being sexually harassed, you have every right to feel angry! The question is, What can you do about it? Plenty! Here are a few suggestions.

**Firmly refuse sexual advances.** Aggressors may assume that a halfhearted no really means yes—or at least maybe—unless you convince them otherwise. So let your no mean no. (Matthew 5:37) If you giggle or act coy, even out of initial embarrassment, it could send the wrong message to the harasser. Be firm and direct. *That is your best defense!*

**Make a scene.** Young Anita says of her harasser: "I had to embarrass him in front of his friends by loudly

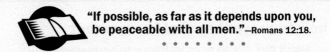

**"If possible, as far as it depends upon you, be peaceable with all men."**—Romans 12:18.

• • • • • • • •

telling him NOT to touch me that way!" The result? "All his friends laughed at him. He was very cold for a while, but a few days later, he apologized for his behavior and later even defended me when someone else tried to bother me."

**If words don't work, walk away.** Better yet, run. And if escape isn't possible, you have the right to fend off molestation. (Deuteronomy 22:25-27) Says one Christian girl, "When a boy tried to grab me, I punched him just as hard as I could, and I ran!"

**Tell someone.** "That's what I finally had to do," admits 16-year-old Adrienne. "I asked my parents for advice on the situation when a boy I thought of as a good friend just wouldn't leave me alone. The more I protested, the more persistent he became, almost as if it were

### ⟩⟩⟩ action plan!

*If someone tries to insult or provoke me, I will*

✎ ....................................................................................

....................................................................................

*To avoid attracting trouble, I will*

....................................................................................

....................................................................................

*What I would like to ask my parent(s) about this subject is*

....................................................................................

....................................................................................

*Tell a sexual harasser to back off!*

a game." Adrienne's parents had practical advice that helped her cope with the problem. No doubt your parents can help you too.

Having to deal with bullying or sexual harassment is no fun. But always remember this: Christian youths need not be helpless victims of bullies; neither should they tolerate or be allured by the advances of a harasser. By taking the steps mentioned, you can deal with these challenges.

**IN OUR NEXT CHAPTER** *Peer pressure is one of the most powerful forces you must deal with. Learn how to face up to it with confidence.*

### WHAT DO YOU THINK?

- How can you project more confidence and poise in your demeanor and thus reduce the likelihood of being bullied?

- What can you do if you're sexually harassed? (Think of some typical scenarios and possible responses.)

- Why should sexual harassment be of serious concern to you?

**15**

# How can I resist peer pressure?

*"At school you're faced with so much—smoking, drugs, sex. You know that what the kids want you to do is stupid. But you get to this point where you feel you just can't chicken out."—Eve.*

IT'S natural to want to be accepted by others. Peer pressure plays on that desire. For example, if you're being raised as a Christian, you know that such things as premarital sex and alcohol abuse are wrong. (Galatians 5:19-21) Many of your peers, though, urge you to join them in these activities. Have they thought about these matters and made their own decision? Not likely. By and large, they

> **"He that is walking with wise persons will become wise, but he that is having dealings with the stupid ones will fare badly."**
> —Proverbs 13:20.

· · · · · · · · ·

have yielded to the influence of others. They want to be accepted, so they allow others to shape what they believe. Do you? Or do you have the courage to stand up for your convictions?

Moses' brother, Aaron, gave in to pressure—at least in one instance. When the Israelites surrounded him and urged him to make a god for them, he did just what they told him to do! (Exodus 32:1-4) Imagine—this was the man who had confronted Pharaoh, boldly declaring God's message to him. (Exodus 7:1, 2, 16) But when his fellow Israelites poured on the pressure, Aaron caved in. Evidently, he found it easier to stand up to the king of Egypt than to stand up to his peers!

What about you? Do you find it hard to stand up for what you know is right? Would you like to be able to resist peer pressure without appearing tense and afraid? You *can!* The key is to see the pressure coming and decide in advance how you will respond to it. The four steps below will help you to do this.

**1. Anticipate.** (Proverbs 22:3) Often, you can see trouble in advance. For example,

---

**DID YOU KNOW...**

Few of your classmates will have any contact with you a year after you leave school. Many may not even remember your name. But your family —and, most of all, Jehovah God—will *always* be interested in your welfare.—Psalm 37:23-25.

---

you see a group of your schoolmates up ahead, and they're smoking. How likely is it that they'll offer you a cigarette? By anticipating the problem, you'll be ready either to avoid it or to confront it.

**2. Think.** (Hebrews 5:14) You might ask yourself, 'How will I feel in the long run if I go along with the crowd?' True, you might gain the temporary approval of your peers. But how will you feel later, when you're with your parents or fellow Christians? Are you willing to sacrifice a clean standing with God just to please your classmates?

**3. Decide.** (Deuteronomy 30:19) Sooner or later, all servants of God have to *choose* either faithfulness and its blessings or unfaithfulness and its bitter consequences. Men like Joseph, Job, and Jesus made the right choice, while Cain, Esau, and Judas chose poorly. Now it's your turn to decide. What will *you* do?

**4. Act.** You might think this is the hardest part. It's not! If you've already thought about the consequences and made up your mind, *stating* your position can be surprisingly easy—and rewarding. (Proverbs 15:23) Don't worry —you don't have to give your peers a Bible lecture. A simple but firm no may suffice. Or to make your nonnegotiable stand clear, you may choose to say:

> TIP
>
> **To boost your courage, read published experiences of Jehovah's modern-day servants who have successfully stood up for what's right.**

*"Count me out!"*

*"I don't do that sort of thing!"*

*"Come on, you know me better than that!"*

The key is to respond promptly and with conviction. If you do, you might be surprised how quickly your peers

READ MORE ABOUT THIS TOPIC IN VOLUME 1, CHAPTER 9

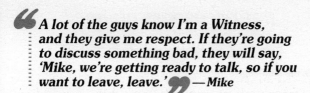

*A lot of the guys know I'm a Witness, and they give me respect. If they're going to discuss something bad, they will say, 'Mike, we're getting ready to talk, so if you want to leave, leave.'* —**Mike**

will back off! Yet, what if they mock you? What if they say, "What's wrong—are you chicken?" Recognize this sort of taunt for what it is—pure peer pressure. How can you respond? You have at least three options.

● You could **absorb** the taunt. (*"You're right, I am scared!"* Then briefly state your reason.)

● You could **deflect** the pressure by stating your position, while not making an issue over it.

● You could **return** the pressure. State your reason for refusing and then appeal to your peers' intellect. (*"I thought you were too smart to smoke!"*)

(Continued on page 135)

## ▶▶▶ action plan!

*I can prepare myself to resist peer pressure by*

✎ .........................................................................................

.........................................................................................

*If my peers attempt to pressure me into wrong conduct, I will*

.........................................................................................

.........................................................................................

*What I would like to ask my parent(s) about this subject is*

.........................................................................................

.........................................................................................

# *peer-pressure planner*

## **1** anticipate

**What is the challenge?** *Smoking cigarettes.*

**Where will I likely face this challenge?** *In the locker room.*

## **2** think

**What will happen if I give in?**
*I will displease Jehovah and my parents. I'll have a bad conscience. It will be harder for me to say no next time.*

**What will happen if I resist?**
*I might get teased or called names. Some of my schoolmates might avoid me. But I will make Jehovah happy, and I will become a stronger person.*

## **3** decide

**If I give in, it will be because**
*I am not prepared well enough to face the peer pressure. I value the approval of my peers more than the approval of Jehovah.*

**I will resist because**
*I know that it displeases Jehovah and that smoking could damage my health.*

## **4** act

**I will**
*say no and walk away.*

---

**peers' taunts**

**If a peer says:** *"Come on, have a cigarette. Or are you too scared?"*
**I could respond to the peer pressure by**

| absorbing it | deflecting it | returning it |
|---|---|---|
| *"You're right. I am scared of cigarettes. I don't want to get lung cancer."* | *"Don't waste your cigarette on me."* | *"No thanks. I thought you were too smart to smoke!"* |

**NOTE: Leave the scene quickly** if your peers continue to pressure you. The longer you stay, the greater the chance that you will become their puppet. Now, fill in your own sheet on the next page.

# peer-pressure planner

Copy this page!

## ① anticipate

What is the challenge? ✎ ..............................................................

Where will I likely face this challenge? ..................................

**② think**

What will happen if I give in?

..............................................................
..............................................................
..............................................................

What will happen if I resist?

..............................................................
..............................................................
..............................................................

If I give in, it will be because . . .

..............................................................
..............................................................
..............................................................

**③ decide**

I will resist because . . .

..............................................................
..............................................................
..............................................................

**④ act**

I will . . .

..............................................................
..............................................................
..............................................................

## peers' taunts

If a peer says: ✎ ..............................................................

I could respond to the peer pressure by

| absorbing it | deflecting it | returning it |
| --- | --- | --- |
| .......... | .......... | .......... |
| .......... | .......... | .......... |
| .......... | .......... | .......... |

Rehearse your responses with a parent or a mature friend.

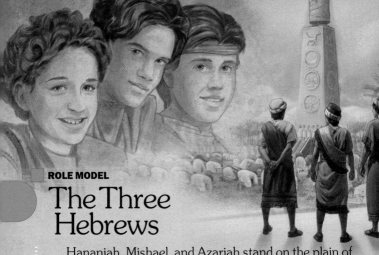

# The Three Hebrews

Hananiah, Mishael, and Azariah stand on the plain of Dura, near Babylon. All around them people bow to the ground before a giant image. **Despite pressure** from their peers and threats from the king, these young men remain resolute. Respectfully but firmly they tell Nebuchadnezzar that their decision to serve Jehovah is **not negotiable**. —Daniel 1:6; 3:17, 18.

These men were youths when exiled to Babylon. Their **faithfulness while young**—refusing to eat foods that may have been forbidden by God's Law—**prepared them** to face difficult challenges later in life. (Daniel 1:6-20) They knew from experience that obeying Jehovah was the wise course. Are you similarly resolved to stick to God's standards despite pressure from your peers? If while you're young you learn to **obey Jehovah** in what might seem to be small matters, you will be better prepared to remain faithful when you face **big challenges** later in life.—Proverbs 3:5, 6; Luke 16:10.

*If you yield to pressure from your peers, you become their puppet*

(Continued from page 131)

If your peers continue to taunt you, *leave the scene!* The longer you stay, the more intense the pressure will become. Even if you have to walk away, remember: *You* took control of the situation. You didn't let your peers squeeze you into their mold!

Some of your peers may taunt you and say that you aren't thinking for yourself. But you are! In fact, Jehovah wants you to *prove* to yourself that it's best to do his will. (Romans 12:2) So why let your peers make you their puppet? (Romans 6:16) Stand up for what you know to be right!

Realistically, you can't hide from peer pressure. But you can know your mind, state your position, and take control. In the end, the choice is yours!—Joshua 24:15.

**IN OUR NEXT CHAPTER** *Living a double life? What good could possibly come from your parents' finding out about it?*

---

**WHAT DO YOU THINK?**

- In what circumstances might the four steps outlined in this chapter prove helpful to you?

- What can happen if you give in to peer pressure?

- What are some ways you can stand up to peer pressure?

**16**

# A double life —who has to know?

- Drinking alcohol
- Associating with people your parents view as bad company
- Listening to debasing music
- Attending rowdy parties
- Dating secretly
- Watching violent or immoral movies or playing violent video games
- Using bad language

LOOK at the list on the previous page. Do you engage in any of those activities behind your parents' backs? If so, you probably know that what you're doing is wrong. You may even suffer the pangs of a guilty conscience. (Romans 2:15) Still, the thought of revealing your misdeeds to your parents isn't a pleasant one. And when you consider the likely consequences, the argument "What my parents don't know won't hurt them" may seem to make sense. But has it occurred to you that your course may amount to living a double life? What might have caused you to act that way?

**The Lure of Independence**

The Bible says that eventually "a man will leave his father and his mother." (Genesis 2:24) The same, of course, can be said of a woman. It's only natural for you to want to grow up, to think for yourself, to make your own decisions. But when parents refuse to give permission for things they consider unwise—or wrong—some youths rebel.

Granted, some parents may seem to be unusually strict. "We can hardly see any movies," complains a young girl named Kim. She adds, "My father has forbidden us to listen to just about any music at all!" Faced with what they see as unreasonable restrictions, some youths begin to feel envious of their peers, who seem to enjoy much more freedom.

A young woman named Tammy identifies another reason why some may live a double life—to fit in with schoolmates. "I started out by using bad language in school," she recalls. "It made me feel I was more like the rest of the kids. Later I tried smoking. I would also drink alcohol to the point of feeling high. Then I started having boyfriends

—secretly because my parents were strict and didn't allow me to date."

A teenage boy named Pete had a similar experience: "I was brought up as one of Jehovah's Witnesses. But I was very afraid of being teased." How did Pete cope with his fear? "I tried to be popular," he says. "I would lie and make excuses as to why I didn't receive any presents during religious holidays." Once Pete began making small compromises, it wasn't long before he engaged in more serious misconduct.

## Nothing Is Hidden

Living a double life is nothing new. Some ancient Israelites tried to get away with it too. However, the prophet Isaiah warned them: "Woe to those who are going very deep in concealing counsel from Jehovah himself, and whose deeds have occurred in a dark place, while they say: 'Who is seeing us, and who is knowing of us?'" (Isaiah 29:15) The Israelites forgot that God saw their deeds. In due time he called them to account for their errors.

**DID YOU KNOW . . .**

Feelings of guilt can be healthy; they can induce a person to correct a wrong course. But a person who persists in sin damages his conscience. It becomes insensitive, like skin that has become seared and then scarred over.
—1 Timothy 4:2.

It's the same today. Even if you successfully hide misconduct from your parents, you cannot hide your actions from the eyes of Jehovah God. "There is not a creation that is not manifest to his sight," says Hebrews 4:13, "but all things are naked and openly exposed to the eyes of him with whom we have an accounting." What, then, is the use of hiding? Re-

**"He that is covering over his transgressions will not succeed, but he that is confessing and leaving them will be shown mercy."**
—Proverbs 28:13.

• • • • • • • • •

member, you can't appease God by simply putting on a show of devotion when you attend religious meetings. Jehovah knows when people 'honor him with their lips, but their hearts are far removed from him.'—Mark 7:6.

Did you realize that those who live a double life grieve Jehovah? Is that really possible? Indeed it is! When the people of ancient Israel abandoned God's Law, "they pained even the Holy One of Israel." (Psalm 78:41) How pained he must be today when youths reared "in the discipline and mental-regulating of Jehovah" secretly do wrong things!—Ephesians 6:4.

## Set Matters Straight

Really, you owe it to God, to your parents, and to yourself to confess to what has been going on in secret. Admittedly, this may result in embarrassment and perhaps some unpleasant consequences. (Hebrews 12:11) For example, if you've carried on a pattern of lying and deception, you've undermined your parents' trust in you. So don't be surprised if for a while they restrict you more than before. Still, coming clean is the best course. Why?

Consider this illustration: Imagine that you and your family are hiking. When your

> **TIP**
>
> Don't minimize your errors, but avoid the trap of pessimism. Remember that Jehovah is ready to forgive.—Psalm 86:5.

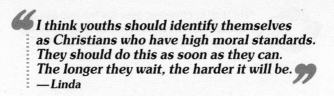

*I think youths should identify themselves as Christians who have high moral standards. They should do this as soon as they can. The longer they wait, the harder it will be.*
—Linda

parents aren't looking, you disobey their order to stay close to them and you wander off the trail, becoming lost. Suddenly, you find yourself sinking in quicksand. Would you be too embarrassed to call for help? Would you worry that your parents might discipline you for ignoring their warnings? No! You would yell as loudly as you could.

Similarly, if you're living a double life, you need help urgently. Remember, you cannot go back and undo the past. But you can alter the future. As painful and difficult as it will no doubt be, it makes sense to call for help before you do any more damage to yourself or to your family. If you're

## ▶▶▶ action plan!

*If I have been living a double life,
I will talk to*

✎ ............................................................................

*I can cope with any discipline I receive by*

............................................................................

............................................................................

*What I would like to ask my parent(s) about this
subject is*

............................................................................

............................................................................

*If you're sinking in the quicksand of a double life, you need to call for help*

truly sorry for your course, Jehovah will be merciful.—Isaiah 1:18; Luke 6:36.

Therefore, tell your parents the truth. Acknowledge their hurt. Accept their discipline. If you do so, you will bring joy to your parents and to Jehovah God. You will also feel the wonderful relief of regaining a clear conscience.—Proverbs 27:11; 2 Corinthians 4:2.

**IN OUR NEXT CHAPTER** *You have a lot in common with your classmates. But what should you know about school friendships?*

**WHAT DO YOU THINK?**

- What motivates some teens to live a double life?
- What are some of the consequences of leading a double life?
- Why is it worth the effort to break free from such a lifestyle?

# 17

# What should I know about school friendships?

*"Sometimes I'd see a group of kids and think, 'Wow, they're really good friends. I want to be part of that.'"*—Joe.

*"I didn't have a problem making friends at school. It was easy. That was my problem."*—Maria.

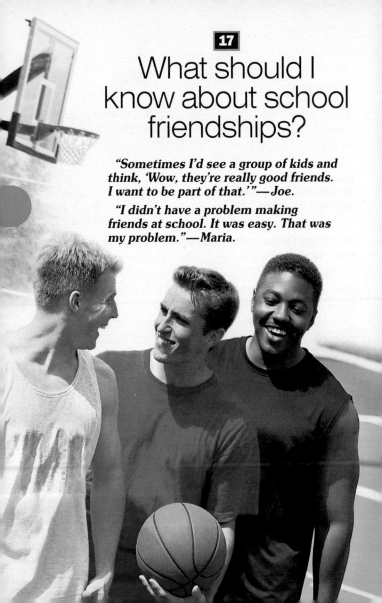

EVERYONE needs friends—people they can relax with during the good times and rely on during the bad. Jesus had friends, and he enjoyed socializing with them. (John 15:15) Then, when he faced death on a torture stake, Jesus' close friend John, "the disciple whom he loved," was nearby. (John 19:25-27; 21:20) You need friends like that—people who will stick with you through thick and thin!

Perhaps you feel that you've found friends like that at school—one or two of your classmates with whom you've hit it off well. You share some similar interests and enjoy talking together. To you they may not seem to fit the category of 'bad association.' (1 Corinthians 15:33) "You see these kids almost every day," says Anne. "So you feel comfortable around them. It's not like being around your spiritual brothers and sisters, where at times you feel you need to be more careful how you act. At school you can relax." In addition, you may find yourself viewing things the way Lois did, who says, "I wanted my school friends to see that Jehovah's Witnesses are not as different as everyone thinks, to show them we're normal." Are those sound reasons to become close friends with your schoolmates?

## Why the Need for Caution?

Consider what happened to Maria, quoted at the outset. Her outgoing nature made it easy for her to attract friends but difficult for her to know where to draw the line.

> *I used to act just like the other kids at school, so it was easy to make friends there. But I learned from my mistakes. Now I have friends inside the congregation —friends I can trust.*—Daniel

> **"I do all things for the sake of the good news, that I may become a sharer of it with others."**
> —1 Corinthians 9:23.

• • • • • • • • •

"I liked being liked, by both girls and boys," she admits. "As a result, I found myself sliding deeper and deeper into the quicksand of this world." Lois experienced something similar. "The attitudes of the other kids rubbed off on me," she says. "I began acting like them."

That outcome isn't surprising. After all, to remain close friends with someone, you need to share that one's interests and values. If you forge close friendships with people who don't adhere to your Scriptural beliefs and standards, such association is bound to affect your conduct. (Proverbs 13:20) For good reason, the apostle Paul wrote: "Do not become unevenly yoked with unbelievers."—2 Corinthians 6:14.

### What You Can Do

Does Paul's counsel mean that you should shun your classmates and remain aloof? No! To fulfill their commission to "make disciples of people of all the nations," Christians need to know how to relate to men and women of all races, religions, and cultures. —Matthew 28:19.

The apostle Paul set an excellent example in this regard. He knew how to converse with "people of all sorts," even though he did not share

**TIP**

If some of your classmates are open to learning about your beliefs, allow them to express their views too. Genuinely listen. When you speak, do so "with a mild temper and deep respect."—1 Peter 3:15.

their beliefs. (1 Corinthians 9: 22, 23) You can follow Paul's example. Be cordial with your peers. Learn to communicate well with them. However, resist the urge to let your speech and conduct conform to that of your classmates. Instead, as soon as possible, respectfully explain to them why you choose to live by Bible standards. —2 Timothy 2:25.

True, you will stand out as different, and this isn't an easy thing to do. (John 15:19) But why not look at the matter this way? If you were in a lifeboat surrounded by people stranded in the water, how could you really help them —by abandoning the boat and jumping in with them? Certainly not!

### ⟫⟫⟫ action plan!

*If I feel that my relationship with a classmate has become too close, I will*

✎ ......................................................................

......................................................................

*If a schoolmate ridicules my beliefs, I will deal with the situation by*

......................................................................

......................................................................

*What I would like to ask my parent(s) about this subject is*

......................................................................

......................................................................

*How can you best help a drowning person —by jumping into the water or by providing a life preserver?*

Similarly, at school you're surrounded by people who lack the protection that comes from being one of Jehovah's friends. (Psalm 121:2-8) If you were to abandon Jehovah's standards just to be close to your classmates, you would only endanger your own spiritual health and happiness. (Ephesians 4:14, 15; James 4:4) How much better it would be if you tried to help your classmates join you in the lifeboat, so to speak, by showing them how to serve Jehovah. Really, in what better way could you prove to be a true friend?

---

**WHAT DO YOU THINK?**

- Why do you think it might seem easier to make friends at school than in the Christian congregation?

- What dangers are there in spending leisure time with an unbelieving classmate after school hours?

- What benefits come from letting your classmates know that you're one of Jehovah's Witnesses?

---

*What situation at school do you find most difficult to deal with?*

*Write about how you plan to handle this problem.*

# MONEY MATTERS 5

As your parents have probably drummed into your head, money doesn't grow on trees. They're right. That's why it's important for you to handle money responsibly. While money serves a vital purpose, it can create stress, damage friendships, and destroy your relationship with God. Certainly, your attitude toward money can have a profound effect on you. **Chapters 18-20** will show you how to maintain a balanced view.

# 18

# How can I make some money?

*"I want money to buy a car."—Sergio.*

*"I like to shop."—Laurie-Ann.*

*"There are some things that are really nice, and I would love to have them; but my parents can't afford them."—Mike.*

YOU may have similar reasons for wanting to get your hands on some money. Or perhaps you need to make money to help support your family. Even if you don't directly contribute to household expenses, paying for your own clothes or other personal items may relieve your parents of some economic pressure.

In any event, obtaining things for yourself or for your family requires money. Although Jesus promised that God

**"No matter how much a lazy person may want something, he will never get it. A hard worker will get everything he wants."**
—Proverbs 13:4, *Today's English Version.*

• • • • • • • •

would provide for those 'seeking first God's Kingdom,' a Christian still needs to take the initiative to provide for himself. (Matthew 6:33; Acts 18:1-3; 2 Thessalonians 3:10) So, how can you make some money? And more important, how can you keep a balanced attitude toward it?

## How to Find a Job

If you really need something that costs more than your parents can afford, you may be able to get a job to earn enough money to buy it yourself. Talk to your parents about the idea. They may be impressed by your initiative. Assuming that they agree and that it's legal for you to work, here are four suggestions that will help you to find employment.

**Spread the word.** Tell your neighbors, teachers, and relatives that you're looking for work. If you're shy about asking them directly, you might simply ask them what work they did when they were your age. The more people who know that you're looking for work, the more leads and referrals you'll likely get.

**Pursue all leads.** Respond to newspaper or Internet want ads and information boards in stores, your school, and other public areas. "That's how I got my job," says a youth named Dave. "I looked in the paper, faxed them a résumé, and called them up." If

**DID YOU KNOW ...**

In some places, up to 85 percent of available jobs aren't advertised.

this doesn't work, perhaps you can convince an employer that he or she needs a service that you can perform.

**Write and distribute a résumé.** On a piece of paper, write down how you can be contacted and list your skills and work experience. You don't think you have anything to list? Think again. Have you ever taken care of a younger sibling when your parents were away, or have you babysat for others? This shows that you're responsible. Have you helped your dad fix the car? Perhaps this shows that you have mechanical aptitude. Do you know how to type or use a computer? Or did you get good marks in school for some innovative project? Those are good selling points for prospective employers. Include them on your résumé. Give your résumé to potential employers, and ask friends and relatives to distribute it to anyone they know who's looking for workers.

**Work for yourself.** Think about your neighborhood. Is there a need for goods or services that no one else is providing? For example, suppose you love animals. You could offer to bathe or trim your neighbors' pets for a fee. Or maybe you play a musical instrument. Could you perhaps teach others to play? Or possibly it's a matter of doing work that others often don't want to do, such as washing windows or cleaning. A Christian isn't embarrassed to work with his hands. (Ephesians 4:28) Of course, being self-employed requires that you be self-motivated, disciplined, and willing to take the initiative.

A word of caution: Don't rush into an enterprise before studying all the costs and factors involved. (Luke 14:28-30)

✔ **TIP**

Send your résumé to companies without waiting for them to advertise a job opening.

READ MORE ABOUT THIS TOPIC IN VOLUME 1, CHAPTER 21

> **If your happiness is always based on owning things, you'll never be happy. There will always be something new that you want. You need to learn to be happy with what you have.** —*Jonathan*

First, talk it over with your parents. Also talk to others who have performed similar work. Will you be required to pay taxes? Will you need to obtain a license or a permit? Check with local authorities for details.—Romans 13:1.

### Keep Your Balance

Imagine trying to ride a bicycle while attempting to carry a number of items, such as a school bag, a ball, and maybe some bags of groceries. The more items you try to carry, the harder it is for you to keep your balance! The same would be true if you were to take on a job that is more than you can handle. Use up too much of your time, energy, and alertness on after-school work, and your health and school grades may suffer. More important, a strenuous work schedule may make it difficult for you to follow the Christian routine of meetings, Bible study, and participation in the Christian ministry. "I have missed meetings because I was tired after a day of school and work," admits a youth named Michèle.

*Taking on too many responsibilities can make it difficult for you to maintain your balance*

Don't let your view of money become unbalanced in that way! Jesus said that real happiness comes to those who are "conscious of their spiritual need." (Matthew 5:3) He also stated: "Even when a person has an abundance his life does not result from the things he possesses." (Luke 12:15) A Christian youth named Maureen has taken that counsel to heart. "I do not want to get entangled in purely materialistic goals," she says. "I just know that my spirituality will be the price I pay if I get caught up in simply making money."

True, in some parts of the world, youths have no choice but to work long hours to help their families survive. If, however, you're not in that situation, why become unbalanced in this regard? According to most experts, working more than 20 hours a week while attending school is excessive and counterproductive. Some suggest devoting no more than eight to ten hours a week to work. Wise King Solomon stated: "Better is a handful of rest than a double handful of hard work and striving after the wind." —Ecclesiastes 4:6.

Remember, "the deceptive power of riches" can choke your interest in spiritual things. (Mark 4:19) So if you do

## >>> action plan!

*I will increase my chances of finding a job by*

✎ ......................................................................................

......................................................................................

*I will limit the amount of time I work to*
............... *hours each week.*

*What I would like to ask my parent(s) about this subject is*

......................................................................................

......................................................................................

## ⟫ respect money—don't love it

In the hands of a skilled chef, a sharp knife is a useful tool. But the same knife in the hands of someone inexperienced or inattentive can cause serious harm. Money is like a sharp knife. If you handle it skillfully, it's a useful tool. But if you're not careful, you can get hurt! For example, the apostle Paul warned against developing a love of money. In their pursuit of wealth, some sacrifice friendships, family relationships, and even their relationship with God. As a result, they 'stab themselves all over with many pains.' (1 Timothy 6:9, 10) The lesson? Learn to use money skillfully. Respect it, but don't love it!

take an after-school job to earn some money, organize your schedule to give spiritual activities priority. Pray to Jehovah God about the matter. He can strengthen you to stand up to the pressures of the situation and can help you to maintain your spiritual balance.

**IN OUR NEXT CHAPTER** *Do you control your money or does it control you? Find out how you can stay in the driver's seat.*

### WHAT DO YOU THINK?

- Why do you need to make some money?

- What challenges will you face if you find a job?

- How can you maintain a balanced view of money?

# 19

# How can I manage my money?

***How often do you feel that you don't have enough money to spend?***
- ❏ Never
- ❏ Sometimes
- ❏ Frequently

***How often do you buy items you can't really afford?***
- ❏ Never
- ❏ Sometimes
- ❏ Frequently

***How often do you buy something you don't need just because it's on sale?***
- ❏ Never
- ❏ Sometimes
- ❏ Frequently

DOES it seem that you never have quite enough money to spend? If you could get your hands on more, you could buy that game you want. If only your wages were higher, you could buy those shoes you "need."

> **"Money is for a protection; but the advantage of knowledge is that wisdom itself preserves alive its owners."**—Ecclesiastes 7:12.

• • • • • • • • •

Or you may face the same dilemma as does Joan, who says: "Sometimes my friends invite me to do things socially that are expensive. I want to be with my friends, having fun. Nobody wants to say, 'Sorry, I can't afford to go.'"

Rather than fret about the money you don't have, why not learn to manage the money that does pass through your hands? You could wait until you leave home to learn how to manage money. But think, Would you jump out of an aircraft without first learning how to use a parachute? True, a person *might* be able to figure it all out while hurtling to the earth. How much better, though, if he learned the basic principles of using the device before jumping out the door!

Similarly, the best time for you to learn to manage money is while you're at home, before the harsh financial realities of life confront you. "Money is for a protection," wrote King Solomon. (Ecclesiastes 7:12) But money will protect you only if you learn how to control your spending. Doing so will boost your confidence and will increase your parents' respect for you.

### Learn the Basics

Have you ever asked your parents to explain what's involved in maintaining your household? For instance, do you know how much it costs to provide light, heat, and water each month or how much it costs to run a car, buy food, or pay the rent or mortgage? Remember,

## ⋙ money talks

**What do you spend your money on? If you regularly spend money helping others, then your money—not just your words—says that you genuinely care about others. (James 2:14-17) By regularly donating money to support true worship, you "honor Jehovah with your valuable things." (Proverbs 3:9) On the other hand, if you always spend your money on your own needs and wants, what does your money say about you?**

you help incur those bills—and if you leave home, *you* will be the one who has to pay the bills. So you might as well know how big your bills are likely to be. Ask your parents if you can see some of the household bills, and listen closely as they explain how they budget for them.

"A wise person will listen and take in more instruction, and a man of understanding is the one who acquires skillful direction," says a Bible proverb. (Proverbs 1:5) Anna asked for skillful direction from her parents. She says, "My father taught me how to make a budget, and he showed me how important it is to be organized in managing family funds."

Meanwhile, Anna's mother taught her other practical lessons. "She showed me the value of comparing prices before buying," Anna says, adding, "Mom could work wonders with a small amount of money." What has been the payoff for Anna? "I am now able to care for my own finances," she says. "I carefully control my spending, so I have the freedom and the peace of mind that come from avoiding unnecessary debt."

## Recognize the Challenges

Admittedly, controlling your spending is easier in theory than in practice, especially if you live at home and receive an allowance or earn money from a job. Why? Because your parents are likely paying most of the bills. As a result, a large percentage of your money may be available for you to spend at will. And spending money can be fun.

A problem may arise, though, if your peers pressure you into spending beyond reasonable limits. Ellena, 21, says: "Among my peers, shopping has become a major form of entertainment. When I'm out with them, there seems to be an unwritten rule that you must spend money if you're going to have fun."

It's natural for you to want to fit in with your friends. But ask yourself, 'Am I spending money with my friends because I can *afford* to or because I feel I *have* to?' Many people spend money in an attempt to boost their reputation with friends and associates. They try to impress others with what they have rather than who they are. This tendency can cause real financial problems for you, especially if you have a credit card. How can you prevent this?

## Take Control

Instead of maxing out your credit card or spending your whole paycheck on one night out, why not try Ellena's solution? "When I go out with friends," she says, "I plan ahead and calculate a limit to my spending. My pay goes

**DID YOU KNOW...**

If you have a balance of $2,000 on your credit card with an interest rate of 18.5 percent and you make only the minimum payments, it will take you 11 years to pay off your debt and will cost you an *extra* $1,934 in interest.

straight into my bank account, and I take out only the amount I need for that outing. I also find it wise to go shopping only with those of my friends who are careful with their money and who will encourage me to shop around and not buy the first thing I see."

Here are some other suggestions you may want to apply if you have a credit card.

● Keep track of your purchases and carefully match them to your monthly statements to be sure that you're charged only for purchases you made.

● Pay your credit-card bill promptly. If possible, pay it in full.

● Be very cautious about giving your credit-card number and expiration date over the phone or online.

● Avoid using your credit card as a means of obtaining quick cash. Cash advances usually incur a higher interest rate.

● Never lend your credit card to anyone, not even a friend.

But wouldn't simply having more money solve all your spending problems? Not likely! To illustrate: If you were driving and did not have control of your car or if you were in the habit of steering with your eyes closed,

*Spending money uncontrollably is like driving blind*

would putting more fuel in your tank make it more likely that you would reach your destination safely? Likewise, if you don't learn how to control your spending, earning more money won't improve your situation.

Maybe you think you already have your money under control. But ask yourself: 'How much money did I spend during the past month? What did I spend it on?' Not sure? Here's how to take control of your spending before your spending takes control of you.

**1. Keep a record.** For at least one month, record the amount of money you receive and the date you receive it. Describe each item you buy and the amount it costs. At the end of the month, add up the amount received and the amount spent.

### ⟩⟩⟩ action plan!

*I can control my spending by*

........................................................................................................

........................................................................................................

*Before I buy something with a credit card, I will*

........................................................................................................

........................................................................................................

*What I would like to ask my parent(s) about this subject is*

........................................................................................................

........................................................................................................

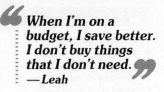

> *When I'm on a budget, I save better. I don't buy things that I don't need.*
> —Leah

**2. Make a budget.** Look at the chart on page 163. In the first column, list all income you expect to receive in a month. In the second column, list how you plan to spend your money; use the entries in your record (step 1) as a guide. As the month progresses, write in the third column the amount you actually spend on each of the planned expenses. Also, record all unplanned spending.

**3. Adjust your habits.** If you're spending more than you anticipated on some items and are accumulating debt, adjust your spending habits. Pay your debts. Stay in control.

Money can be a useful servant if it's used properly. In fact, in most cultures, making and managing money is an important part of life. But try to keep a balanced attitude. "Money has its place, but it is not everything," says a youth named Matthew. "It should never be put ahead of our family or Jehovah."

**IN OUR NEXT CHAPTER** *Is your family poor? If so, how can you make the most of your circumstances?*

---

**WHAT DO YOU THINK?**

- Why should you learn to manage money while you're still living at home?

- Why might you find it difficult to manage your money?

- In what ways can you use your money to help others?

## :: my monthly budget

| | budget for expenses | actual amount spent |
|---|---|---|

**FOOD**

**CLOTHES**

**PHONE**

**ENTERTAINMENT**

**DONATIONS**

**SAVINGS**

**OTHER**

| income |
|---|

ALLOWANCE

PART-TIME JOB

OTHER

| total $ | total $ | total $ |
|---|---|---|

## ⠸ should I live abroad?

Some youths want to live abroad to earn money either for themselves or to support their family. Others move to learn a foreign language, to further their education, or to run away from problems at home. Some Christian youths have moved to lands where there's a need for evangelizers. The decision to move to a foreign land is a big one and should not be taken lightly. Therefore, if you're thinking of living abroad, read and meditate on the scriptures listed below. Ask yourself the questions, and write your answers on a sheet of paper. Then prayerfully make your decision.

☐ *What legal requirements are involved?*—Romans 13:1.

☐ *What will be the total financial cost of moving abroad?*
—Luke 14:28.

☐ *What am I doing now that proves that I would be able to care for my own physical needs when abroad?*
—Proverbs 13:4.

☐ *What advice have I received from mature people who have lived abroad?*—Proverbs 1:5.

☐ *What do my parents think of the idea?*—Proverbs 23:22.

☐ *What's my motive for wanting to move abroad?*
—Galatians 6:7, 8.

☐ *If I'm going to live with others, will they encourage me to maintain good spiritual habits?*—Proverbs 13:20.

☐ *What moral, physical, and spiritual dangers might I face?*—Proverbs 5:3, 4; 27:12; 1 Timothy 6:9, 10.

☐ *Realistically, what benefits do I expect to gain from living abroad?*—Proverbs 14:15.

## 20

# What if my family is poor?

*Gregory, a youth in Eastern Europe, can't afford the clothes or electronic goods some Western youths can. He's so frustrated with his living conditions that he's about to move to Austria. Do you think Gregory is poor?*

☐ Yes  ☐ No

*Thousands of miles away lives Loyiso, a youth from a rural village in southern Africa. Dwelling in a small hut with his family, Loyiso envies the youths in a nearby town who enjoy marvelous "luxuries"—running water and electricity. Would you say that Loyiso is poor?*

☐ Yes  ☐ No

CLEARLY, "poor" is a relative term, meaning different things in various lands. For example, Gregory may have thought of himself as poverty-stricken, but compared with Loyiso he lives in luxury. It's sobering to realize that no matter how poor you may be, others are likely worse off than you are. Still, when you don't have decent clothes to wear to school or when you lack such basics as running water, it may give you little comfort to be told that others have less.

Some youths who grow up poor feel worthless and inferior, and they try to dull their senses with alcohol or drugs. However, efforts to escape from reality only make matters

What if my family is poor?  **165**

# The Poor Widow

Jesus is watching the rich drop contributions into the temple treasury chest. In the crowd he notices a needy widow who donates **"two small coins** of very little value." (Luke 21:2) Jesus praises her act of generosity. Why? Because the others had donated "out of their surplus, but she, out of her want, dropped in all of what she had, her **whole living."**—Mark 12:44.

Do you have the same priorities as this woman did? Are you willing to spend your time and money in serving God? Like the needy widow, you can donate toward the **maintenance** of places of worship. You can also spend your time and money **helping others** learn about Jehovah God. Jehovah noticed and appreciated the small amount the widow gave in his service. God will also appreciate and help you if your **top priority** is to do his will. —Matthew 6:33.

worse. Those who abuse alcohol discover that "it bites just like a serpent, and it secretes poison just like a viper." (Proverbs 23:32) Maria, a girl from a poor single-parent family in South Africa, says, "Trying to escape reality causes more problems than it solves."

You may not turn to drinking or drugs, but you may see little hope of ever improving your lot in life. Where can you turn? The Bible's wise counsel can be like a key that frees you from the shackles of despair, enabling you to cultivate a healthy attitude. Let's see how.

*The Bible's advice can be like a key that frees you from the shackles of despair*

### Examine Your Assets

One positive step you can take is to focus, not on the things you lack, but on the things you *have*. Assets such as a home and a loving family certainly are more valuable than money! A Bible proverb says: "Better is a dish of vegetables where there is love than a manger-fed bull and hatred along with it." (Proverbs 15:17) Christian youths have an especially valuable asset—the support of "the whole association of brothers."—1 Peter 2:17.

Perhaps you can also try viewing your material possessions in a more positive light. Granted, you may live in a simple, perhaps even primitive, home. You may wear old, worn, or patched clothing. And you may long for a more varied diet. But do you need stylish clothes or an elaborate home to please God? Do you need fancy meals to stay alive and in good health? Not really. The apostle Paul learned a valuable lesson in this regard. He experienced both riches and poverty. (Philippians 4:12) His conclusion? "If we have

> *Although I felt trapped by poverty, I realized that joining a gang or stealing for a living would not help at all. Today, many of those from my age group who did those things are either hopeless dropouts, slaves to drink and drugs, or in jail.* —George

food and clothes, that should be enough for us."—1 Timothy 6:8, *Today's English Version.*

Eldred, a South African man who grew up in a family of little means, says: "We just accepted that the family was living on a tight budget and that we could not get all we wanted." Eldred recalls that when his school trousers became threadbare, his mother simply patched them up—again and again and again! "I had to endure a bit of teasing," admits Eldred. "But the main thing was that our clothes were clean and functional."

## Build Self-Respect

James, 11, lived with his mother and his sister in a squatter camp near Johannesburg, South Africa. Materially, they owned almost nothing. However, James still had valuable assets—time and energy—and he enjoyed using these to help others. Each weekend, James volunteered his services to assist in building a local Kingdom Hall of Jehovah's Witnesses. This work not only absorbed time that would have otherwise hung heavy on his hands but also gave him a sense of accomplishment and

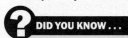

**? DID YOU KNOW...**

Applying Bible principles can help you to cultivate contentment despite your circumstances. —Philippians 4:12, 13; 1 Timothy 6:8; Hebrews 13:5.

a feeling of self-respect. "After a day of hall building, I have this deep feeling of contentment inside!" he says.

**TIP** ✓

Shun gambling, smoking, and the abuse of alcoholic beverages. If other family members have these habits, set an example for them by your conduct.

Another productive activity is the door-to-door Bible education work. (Matthew 24:14) Youths among Jehovah's Witnesses engage in that work on a regular basis. By doing so they give others hope of a better life in the future, and they also increase their own feelings of self-respect and dignity. True, they don't make money from doing such work. But recall the message Jesus gave to Christians in the ancient congregation of Smyrna. They were quite poor materially. Nevertheless, because of their deep spirituality, Jesus could say to them: "I know your tribulation and poverty —but you are rich." Ultimately, because of their actively exercising faith in Jesus' shed blood, they would become

## ▶▶▶ action plan!

*My assets are*

✎ .......................................................................................................................................

.......................................................................................................................................

*I will use these assets to help others by*

.......................................................................................................................................

.......................................................................................................................................

*What I would like to ask my parent(s) about this subject is*

.......................................................................................................................................

.......................................................................................................................................

**"Even when a person has an abundance his life does not result from the things he possesses."**—Luke 12:15.

• • • • • • • • •

supremely rich, receiving the crown of immortal life.—Revelation 2:9, 10.

### Look Ahead

You can develop a close relationship with Jehovah whether you are rich or poor. The Bible states: "The rich one and the one of little means have met each other. The Maker of them all is Jehovah." (Proverbs 22:2) That fact has helped thousands of young Witnesses of Jehovah to cope with poverty. They appreciate that happiness depends, not on owning material things, but on making friends with Jehovah God, who welcomes all who want to serve him. God offers the hope of life in a future new world that will be free of grinding poverty.—2 Peter 3:13; Revelation 21:3, 4.

In the meantime, use your resources wisely. Look to the future. Lay up spiritual treasures. (Matthew 6:19-21) View poverty as a challenge that you *can* cope with!

---

**WHAT DO YOU THINK?**

- Why is "poor" a relative term?
- Why is it unwise to use drugs, alcohol, or other substances to escape from reality?
- What practical steps can you take to cope with poverty?

---

*my journal*

*Describe your biggest money problem.*

_____

_____

_____

_____

_____

_____

*How can you use the information in this section to help you
handle this problem in the future?*

_____

_____

_____

_____

_____

_____

_____

# YOUR PARENTS 6

Parents have the benefit of hindsight. They've already navigated the maze of physical and emotional changes that are part of adolescence. Ideally, they should be in the best position to guide *you* through the maze. Sometimes, though, parents can seem to be part of the problem—not the solution. For example, you might face one of the following challenges:

❏ My parents never stop criticizing me.

❏ My dad or mom is addicted to drugs or alcohol.

❏ My parents are always arguing.

❏ My parents have separated.

**Chapters 21-25** will help you deal with these and other problems.

**21**

# How can I deal with criticism?

"My mother seemed like a police detective —always looking for areas where I failed. Before I had time to finish my chores, she would inspect my work, looking for mistakes."—Craig.

"My parents were always lecturing me about something. They said I just couldn't seem to get my act together. School, home, congregation —they just wouldn't give me a break."—James.

DOES it seem as though nothing you do is ever good enough for your parents? Do you feel that your every move is being examined under a microscope—that you're always being watched and constantly critiqued but you never pass inspection?

### *Which of the following do you hear most often?*

✎ ❏ Your room is always a mess.  ❏ You stay up too late.
   ❏ You watch too much TV.  ❏ You never get up on time.

On the following line, write the parental reminder or criticism that bothers you the most.

✎ .................................................................................

True, commands and criticism may get on your nerves. But consider the alternative: If you never received counsel or discipline, wouldn't you wonder if your parents cared about you? (Hebrews 12:8) Really, discipline is evidence of your parents' love. The Bible says that a father will reprove "a son in whom he finds pleasure."—Proverbs 3:12.

You can be grateful, then, that your parents care enough about you to set you straight! After all, you're young and relatively inexperienced. Sooner or later, correction will be in order. Without guidance, you could easily be overpowered by "the desires incidental to youth."—2 Timothy 2:22.

## But It Hurts!

Of course, "no discipline seems for the present to be joyous, but grievous." (Hebrews 12:11) This is particularly so when you're young. And no wonder! Your personality is in its developing stages. You're still growing up and discovering who you are. So criticism—even when carefully thought out and delivered in a kind way—may trigger resentment.

This reaction is understandable, because the value you place on yourself can easily be influenced by what others say about you. And your parents' opinion in particular greatly affects your sense of self-worth. So when a parent corrects you or complains about the way you do something, it can be devastating.

Should you conclude that *nothing* you do is ever good enough or that you're a complete failure simply because your parents have pointed out a few of your flaws? No. All humans fall woefully short of perfection. (Ecclesiastes 7: 20) And making mistakes is part of the learning process. (Job 6:24) What, though, if your parents seem to have a lot to say when you do something wrong but little to say when you do something right? That can hurt. Still, it hardly means you're a total failure.

## Behind the Criticism

Sometimes a parent might seem overly critical, not because of any particular failing on your part, but simply because he or she is in a bad mood. Has your mom had a hard day? Is she struggling with an illness? Then she might be more prone than usual to pick on you if your room isn't in tip-top shape. Is your dad angry and frustrated over family finances? Then he might speak thoughtlessly "as with the stabs of a sword." (Proverbs 12:18) Granted, such unfair criticism is irritating. But instead of dwelling on the injustice—which will only make you more upset—try to overlook your parents' faults. Re-

**DID YOU KNOW . . .**

**Some dads and moms find it difficult to deal lovingly with their children because they didn't receive adequate love and understanding from their own parents.**

> *All my life it was my mother yelling and me answering her back. But now I try to put into practice what God's Word says. It works. Mom's attitude has started to change. By applying the Bible, I came to understand her better. Our relationship improved.* —Marleen

member: "We all stumble many times. If anyone does not stumble in word, this one is a perfect man."—James 3:2.

As imperfect humans, parents too can be afflicted with feelings of inadequacy. In fact, failure on your part can make them feel as if *they* have failed. For example, a mother might criticize her daughter when she brings home a poor report card from school. But what the mother might actually be thinking is, 'I'm afraid that I'm failing as a mother because I'm not motivating my daughter to succeed.'

### Keeping Cool When Under Fire

Whatever is behind the criticism, the question is, How can you cope with it? First, be careful not to lash out. Proverbs 17:27 says: "Anyone holding back his sayings is possessed of knowledge, and a man of discernment is cool of spirit." How can you remain "cool of spirit" when under fire? Try the following:

**Listen.** Rather than being quick to justify your actions or protest your innocence, try to hold back your emotions and absorb what your parents have to say. The disciple James told Christians to be "swift about hearing, slow about speaking, slow about wrath." (James 1:19) If you angrily interrupt while your parents are talking to you, they'll think that you aren't listening. This will frustrate them and inevitably lead to *more* counsel, not *less*.

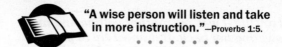

**"A wise person will listen and take in more instruction."**—Proverbs 1:5.

• • • • • • • • •

**Focus.** At times, you may feel that your parents' counsel was delivered in a less-than-kind manner. Rather than dwell on *the way* they spoke to you, though, focus on *what* was said. Ask yourself: 'What part of this criticism do I know to be true? Have I heard my parents complain about this matter before? What would it cost me to comply with their wishes?' Remember, despite how it may seem at the moment, your parents' concern is motivated by love. If they really did hate you, they wouldn't discipline you at all. —Proverbs 13:24.

**Rephrase.** If you rephrase your parents' counsel and repeat it back to them in a respectful manner, you reassure them that you heard what they said. For example, a parent might say: "You always leave your room in a mess. If you don't clean it up, you're grounded!" Now, your room may look just fine to you. But expressing that thought will hardly be helpful. Try to look at things from your parents' viewpoint. It would be better to say, without sarcasm, something like this: "You're right. My room *is* messy. Would you like me to clean it right now or after dinner?" When you acknowledge your parents' concerns in this way, the tension is more likely to ease. Of course, you then

**TIP**

To help you accept correction from your parents

● Appreciate any commendation that you receive with the criticism.

● Ask for clarification if you're not clear about the problem or the expected solution.

need to follow through on your parents' direction.—Ephesians 6:1.

**Wait.** Save any justification until after you've complied with your parents' wishes. "The one keeping his lips in check is acting discreetly," says the Bible. (Proverbs 10:19) Once your parents see that you really were listening to them, they'll be far more inclined to listen to you.

Write here which of the above four steps you need to work on most. ✎ ...................................................................

### Why It's Worth the Effort

Would you be willing to endure some physical hardship to discover a fortune in gold? Well, the Bible says that wisdom is worth far more than any treasure. (Proverbs 3: 13, 14) How do you become wise? Proverbs 19:20 says: "Listen to counsel and accept discipline, in order that you may become wise in your future." True, counsel and discipline may cause some discomfort. But if you find and

### >>> action plan!

*The next time my parents criticize me, I will*

✎ ...........................................................................................

...........................................................................................

*If I feel that my parents are being overly critical, I will*

...........................................................................................

...........................................................................................

*What I would like to ask my parent(s) about this subject is*

...........................................................................................

...........................................................................................

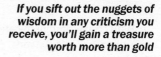

*If you sift out the nuggets of wisdom in any criticism you receive, you'll gain a treasure worth more than gold*

apply the nuggets of wisdom in any criticism you receive, you'll gain a treasure worth more than gold.

Let's face it: Criticism is part of life. You already have to cope with it from your parents and teachers. In the future, you will no doubt have employers and others to deal with. Learn how to handle criticism at home, and you'll become a progressive student, a valued employee, and a more confident person in general. Surely, it's worth enduring a little criticism to gain those results!

**IN OUR NEXT CHAPTER** *Hemmed in by house rules? Learn how to be content with the freedom you have—and even how you might gain more.*

**WHAT DO YOU THINK?**

- Why might you find it hard to accept criticism?
- What may prompt your parents to be critical of you?
- How can you make the most of any counsel you receive?

# 22

# Why so many rules?

Name some rules that
exist in your family. ✎.............................................

...............................................

Do you think family
rules are always fair? ☐ Yes   ☐ No

Which rule do you find the
most difficult to obey? ...............................................

HOUSE RULES, as they're sometimes called, are the dos and don'ts that your parents have set for you. Such rules may include requirements about homework, chores, and curfews, as well as restrictions on your use of the phone, the TV, and the computer. Some rules may extend beyond the walls of your home to include your behavior at school and your choice of friends.

Do you feel hemmed in by these restrictions? Perhaps you can relate to the following youths:

*"My curfew used to drive me crazy! I hated it when others were allowed to stay out later than I was."*—Allen.

*"It's horrible having your cell-phone calls monitored. I feel that I'm being treated like a child!"*—Elizabeth.

*"I felt that my parents were trying to wreck my social life, as though they didn't want me to have any friends!"*—Nicole.

While young people often find themselves on the wrong side of their parents' rules, most youths acknowledge that some regulations are needed to prevent total chaos. But if house rules are necessary, why are some of them so annoying?

### "I'm Not a Baby Anymore!"

Perhaps you chafe at rules because you feel that you're being treated like a child. You want to cry out, "I'm not a baby anymore!" Of course, your parents probably feel that their rules are vital if they are to protect you and prepare you for the responsibilities of adulthood.

Still, it might seem as if the rules in your home have not "grown up" as much as you have. You might feel restricted, as did a girl named Brielle, who said of her parents: "They have completely forgotten what it's like to be

> **When you're young, you tend to think you know everything. So when your parents restrict you, it's easy to get upset with them. But their rules are really for the best.** —Megan

my age. They don't want me to have my say, make a choice, or be an adult." A youth named Allison feels similarly. "My parents don't seem to understand that I'm 18 years old and not 10," she says. "They need to trust me more!"

House rules can be especially painful to submit to if your siblings seem to be given more lenient treatment. For example, recalling his teen years, a young man named Matthew says of his younger sister and his cousins, "The girls got away with 'murder'!"

### No Rules?

Understandably, you may long for a life out from under your parents' authority. But would you really be better off without their restrictions? You probably know youths your age who can stay out as late as they want, can wear anything they like, and can go with their friends whenever and wherever it suits them. Perhaps the parents are simply too busy to notice what their children are doing. In any case, the Bible shows that this approach to child-rearing will not be successful. (Proverbs

**DID YOU KNOW...**

Research shows that youths whose parents lovingly enforce rules are more likely to excel academically, to interact well with others, and to be happy.

29:15) The lack of love you see in the world is largely due to its self-centered people, many of whom were raised in homes without restraint.—2 Timothy 3:1-5.

Rather than envying youths who are allowed to do as they please, try to see your parents' rules as evidence of their love and concern for you. By enforcing reasonable limits, they're imitating Jehovah God, who said to his people: "I shall make you have insight and instruct you in the way you should go. I will give advice with my eye upon you."—Psalm 32:8.

At times, though, you may feel overwhelmed by your parents' rules. How can you gain some relief?

## Communication That Works

Whether you want to gain more freedom or just reduce your frustration with the limits your parents now place on you, the key is good communication. 'But I've *tried* talking to my parents, and it just doesn't work!' some might say. If that's how you feel, ask yourself, 'Could I improve my communication skills?' Communication is a vital tool that can (1) help others to understand you or (2) help you to understand why what you want is being refused. Really, if you want to receive grown-up privileges, it's only reasonable that you develop mature communication skills. How can you do so?

**Learn to control your emotions.** Good communication requires self-control. The Bible states: "All his spirit is

**TIP**

If you want your parents to give you more freedom, first build a record of abiding by their rules. When you have a track record of being obedient, they'll be more likely to grant your requests.

*Obeying your parents' rules is like paying off a debt to the bank —the more reliable you are, the more trust (or credit) you will receive*

what a stupid one lets out, but he that is wise keeps it calm to the last." (Proverbs 29:11) So avoid whining, sulking, and throwing childish tantrums. Admittedly, you may feel like slamming the door or stomping around the house when your parents restrict you. However, such behavior will probably lead to more rules—not to more freedom.

**Try to see your parents' point of view.** Tracy, a Christian youth in a single-parent family, says, "I ask myself, 'What is my mother trying to accomplish with her rules?'" Tracy's conclusion? "She's trying to help me become a better person." (Proverbs 3:1, 2) Showing such empathy may help you to communicate effectively with your parents.

For example, suppose your parents are reluctant to let you attend a certain gathering. Instead of arguing, you could ask, "What if a mature, trustworthy friend came along with me?" Your parents may still not grant your

## ⁘ is it really favoritism?

Have you ever wondered, 'Why can't parents treat everyone exactly the same?' If so, consider this fact: Equal treatment isn't always fair, and fair treatment isn't always equal. Really, the question is, Are *your* needs being neglected? For instance, when you need your parents' advice, help, or support, are they there for you? If so, can you honestly say that you're the victim of injustice? Since you and your siblings are individuals with different needs, it just isn't possible for your parents to treat all of you the same way all the time. That's what Beth came to appreciate. Now 18, she says: "My brother and I are two different people and need to be treated differently. Looking back, I can't believe I couldn't see that when I was younger."

request. But if you understand their concerns, you have a better chance of suggesting an acceptable option.

**Build your parents' confidence in you.** Imagine a man who owes money to a bank. If he makes his payments regularly, he'll earn the bank's trust and the bank may even extend more credit to him in the future. It's similar at home. You owe your parents your obedience. If you prove trustworthy—even in small things—your parents are likely to trust you more in the future. Of course, if you continually let your parents down, don't be surprised if they reduce or even close your "line of credit."

### When a Rule Has Been Broken

Sooner or later, you're likely to cross the line—fail to do your chores, talk too long on the phone, or miss a cur-

READ MORE ABOUT THIS TOPIC IN VOLUME 1, CHAPTER 3

few. (Psalm 130:3) Then you'll have to face your parents! How can you keep a bad situation from getting worse?

**Speak the truth.** Do not tell tall tales. If you do, that would only undermine any remaining trust your parents have in you. So be honest and specific about details. (Proverbs 28:13) Avoid justifying or minimizing what happened. And always remember that "an answer, when mild, turns away rage."—Proverbs 15:1.

**Apologize.** Expressing regret over the worry, disappointment, or extra work you caused is appropriate and may reduce the severity of your punishment. However, your sorrow must be sincere.

**Accept the consequences.** (Galatians 6:7) Your first response may be to dispute the punishment, especially if it

⟫⟫⟫ **action plan!**

If I break a house rule, I will say

✎ ..................................................................................................

..................................................................................................

I can build my parents' trust in me by

..................................................................................................

..................................................................................................

What I would like to ask my parent(s) about this subject is

..................................................................................................

..................................................................................................

**"Honor your father and your mother . . .
that it may go well with you."**
—Ephesians 6:2, 3.

• • • • • • • •

seems unfair. However, taking responsibility for your actions is a sign of maturity. Your best option may simply be to work at regaining your parents' confidence.

Write here which of the above three points you need to work on most. ✎...................................................................

Remember, your parents have the responsibility to exercise reasonable control over your actions. Thus, the Bible speaks of "the commandment of your father" and "the law of your mother." (Proverbs 6:20) Nevertheless, you need not feel that house rules will ruin your life. On the contrary, if you submit to your parents' authority, Jehovah promises that, in the long run, it will "go well with you"!—Ephesians 6:1-3.

**IN OUR NEXT CHAPTER** *Do you have a parent who is addicted to drugs or alcohol? Find out how you can cope.*

**WHAT DO YOU THINK?**

- Why might your parents seem overly protective of you at times?

- Why do you sometimes overreact to restrictions?

- How can you improve your communication with your parents?

## ❖ talk to your parents!

The preceding two chapters have discussed how you can deal with parental criticism and house rules. What if you feel that your parents are being too harsh in either or both of these areas? How could you open up a discussion with them about it?

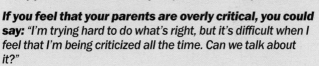

● Pick a time when you're relaxed and your parents aren't too busy.

● Speak from the heart, but don't be ruled by your emotions. Accord your parents due respect.

*If you feel that your parents are overly critical, you could say:* "I'm trying hard to do what's right, but it's difficult when I feel that I'm being criticized all the time. Can we talk about it?"

Write below how *you* would open up a discussion with your parents about this subject.

✎ ......................................................................

✔ **TIP:** Use Chapter 21 to break the ice. Perhaps your parents will be willing to discuss the material in that chapter with you.

*If you feel that your parents are not allowing you enough freedom, you could say:* "I'd like to show myself more responsible so that in time I can be granted more freedom. What do you think I should work on?"

Write below how *you* could open up a discussion with your parents about this subject.

✎ ......................................................................

✔ **TIP:** Review Chapter 3 in Volume 1. It's entitled "How Can I Get My Folks to Give Me More Freedom?" Then make a list of any questions you may have about what you read.

# 23

# What if my parent is addicted to drugs or alcohol?

*"Dad said he'd be away working on the van, but we hadn't heard from him all day. Mom tried calling him on the phone. No answer. A little while later, I noticed that Mom had a worried look on her face and that she was getting ready to leave. 'I'm going to check on your dad,' she told me.*

*"Later, Mom returned—alone. 'Dad wasn't there, was he?' I asked. 'No,' she replied.*

*"At that moment I knew that Dad was up to his old tricks. It was just like the last time. You see, my dad's a drug addict. And by the time he came home, my Mom and I were nervous wrecks. I basically ignored him all the next day—which I feel absolutely horrible about."—Karen, 14.*

MILLIONS of youths endure the daily turmoil of living with a parent who's hooked on drugs or alcohol. If one of your parents is enslaved to such an addiction, he or she may embarrass, frustrate, and even anger you.

Mary, for example, was raised by a dad who seemed to be a nice person when in public. But he was a closet alcoholic, and at home he subjected his family to profanity and abuse. "People would come up to us children and tell us what a wonderful father we had and how fortunate we were," Mary recalls bitterly.*

If one of your parents is addicted to alcohol or drugs, how can you cope?

## Behind the Addiction

First of all, it helps to gain some insight into your parent's problem. "A man of understanding is the one who acquires skillful direction," says Proverbs 1:5. So it would be good for you to learn something about what addiction is, who gets addicted to alcohol or drugs, and why.

For instance, an alcoholic isn't simply someone who overdrinks on occasion. On the contrary, he has a chronic drinking disorder.# He's preoccupied—even obsessed—with alcohol and cannot control his consumption of it once he starts drinking. His addiction causes painful problems affecting his family, work, and health.

While certain people may be physically prone to alcohol addiction, emotional factors also appear to be involved. In fact, many alcoholics often harbor negative

---

* If you're being mistreated by an alcoholic parent, you would do well to seek help. Confide in an adult you trust. If you're one of Jehovah's Witnesses, you could approach a congregation elder or another mature Christian.

# Although we refer to the alcoholic or addict as a male, the principles discussed also apply to females.

feelings about themselves. (Proverbs 14:13) Some of them, in fact, grew up in families where their own parents were alcoholics. For such people, drinking may numb the pain of childhood emotional scars. The same factors might be involved when a person is addicted to drugs.

Of course, drinking or taking drugs only compounds a person's problems; his thinking and emotions now become even more warped. That's why your parent may need considerable help from a trained professional to break free from his addiction.

### Modifying Your Expectations

Granted, understanding why your parent behaves so badly doesn't make the problem disappear. Still, having some insight into his addiction might allow you to view your parent with a measure of compassion.

**? DID YOU KNOW...**

In the Bible "honor" can simply mean recognizing legitimate authority. (Ephesians 6:1, 2) Hence, honoring a parent doesn't require that you always approve of his course of behavior.

For example, would you expect a parent with a broken leg to play a game of soccer with you? What if you knew that the injury was the result of your parent's own foolish actions? No doubt, you'd be disappointed. Nevertheless, you would realize that until the

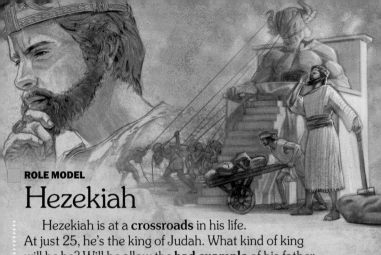

# Hezekiah

Hezekiah is at a **crossroads** in his life. At just 25, he's the king of Judah. What kind of king will he be? Will he allow the **bad example** of his father, King Ahaz, to influence him? Right up to his death, Ahaz had been an **unrepentant apostate.** He promoted pagan worship and even burned at least one of Hezekiah's brothers on a pagan altar. (2 Chronicles 28:1-4) However, Hezekiah doesn't permit his father's hypocritical conduct to sour him on the worship of Jehovah, nor does he feel doomed to repeat his father's mistakes. Instead, Hezekiah keeps **"sticking to Jehovah."**—2 Kings 18:6.

Does one of your parents mock the worship of Jehovah? Is he or she abusive or a slave to some bad habit? If so, you **don't have to repeat** your parent's mistakes! Hezekiah didn't let his sad family background ruin his life. In fact, he became such a good king that "after him there proved to be no one like him among all the kings of Judah." (2 Kings 18:5) Like Hezekiah, you can make a **success** of your life despite difficult family circumstances. How? Keep "sticking to Jehovah."

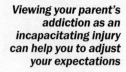

*Viewing your parent's addiction as an incapacitating injury can help you to adjust your expectations*

injury heals, your parent's ability to play ball with you would be severely limited. Grasping that fact would help you to adjust your expectations.

Similarly, an alcoholic parent or one who is addicted to drugs is emotionally and mentally crippled. True, the "injury" is self-inflicted. And you may rightly resent your parent's foolish conduct. However, until your parent seeks help to heal his addiction, he'll be severely limited in his ability to care for you. Viewing his addiction as an incapacitating injury may help you to modify your expectations.

## What You Can Do

The fact remains that until your parent straightens out his life, you must live with the consequences of his behavior. In the meantime, what can you do about it?

**Don't take responsibility for your parent's addiction.** Your parent—and your parent alone—is responsible for his addiction. "Each one will carry his own load," says Galatians 6:5. It's not your job, then, to cure your parent, nor are you obliged to shield him from the consequences of his addiction. For example, you don't have to

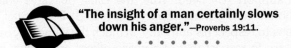

**"The insight of a man certainly slows down his anger."**—Proverbs 19:11.

• • • • • • • • •

lie for him to his boss or drag him off the front porch when he's fallen into a drunken stupor there.

**Encourage your parent to get help.** Your parent's biggest problem may be admitting that he *has* a problem. When he's sober and calm, perhaps the nonaddicted parent along with the older siblings can tell him how his behavior is affecting the family and what he needs to do about it.

In addition, your addicted parent might do well to write down the answers to the following questions: *What will happen to me and my family if I keep drinking or taking drugs? What will happen if I give up my habit? What must I do to get help?*

**If trouble is brewing, leave the scene.** "Before the quarrel has burst forth, take your leave," says Proverbs 17:14. Don't put yourself at risk by getting in the middle of a quarrel. If possible, retire to your room or go to a friend's house. When the threat of violence exists, outside help may be needed.

**Acknowledge your feelings.** Some youths feel guilty because they resent an addicted parent. It's only normal to feel a degree of resentment, especially if your parent's addiction prevents him from giving you the love

> **TIP** ✔
>
> Rather than hate your parent, develop a healthy hatred of your parent's wrongdoing.
> —Proverbs 8:13; Jude 23.

and support you need. True, the Bible obligates you to honor your parent. (Ephesians 6:2, 3) But "honor" means to respect his authority, in much the same way as you are to respect that of a police officer or a judge. It doesn't mean that you approve of your parent's addiction. (Romans 12:9) Nor are you a bad person because you're repulsed by his drinking or drug abuse; after all, substance abuse *is* repulsive!—Proverbs 23:29-35.

**Find upbuilding association.** When life at home is chaotic, you can lose sight of what's normal. It's important, therefore, that you enjoy the association of people who are spiritually and emotionally healthy. Members of the Christian congregation can provide much nurturing and support as well as an occasional break from family stress. (Proverbs 17:17) Association with Christian families can give you a healthy model of family life to counteract the distorted model you observe at home.

## ▶▶▶ action plan!

*If my parent becomes verbally or physically abusive, I will*

✎ ....................................................................................

....................................................................................

*I can encourage my parent to get help by*

....................................................................................

....................................................................................

*What I would like to ask my parent(s) about this subject is*

....................................................................................

....................................................................................

**Seek help for yourself.** Having a mature, trusted adult with whom you can share your feelings really helps. Congregation elders are willing to help you when you need them. The Bible says that these men can be "like a hiding place from the wind and a place of concealment from the rainstorm, like streams of water in a waterless country, like the shadow of a heavy crag in an exhausted land." (Isaiah 32:2) So don't be afraid or ashamed to go to them for comfort and advice.

Write here which of the above six steps you will try to apply first. ✎ ..................................................................

You may not be able to change the situation at home, but you can change the way you're affected by it. Rather than trying to control your parent, focus on the one person you can control—*you.* "Keep working out *your own* salvation," wrote the apostle Paul. (Philippians 2:12) Doing so will help you maintain a positive outlook, and it might even prod your parent to seek help for his addiction.

**IN OUR NEXT CHAPTER** *What if your parents seem to argue all the time? How can you cope with the emotional turmoil?*

---

**WHAT DO YOU THINK?**

- What causes some people to become addicted to alcohol or drugs?

- Why are you not responsible for your parent's addiction?

- What aspects of your situation can you control, and how can you do so?

## if a parent stops serving Jehovah

If one of your parents stops living by Bible standards —perhaps even makes known that he no longer wants to be part of the Christian congregation—what can you do?

● Realize that Jehovah doesn't hold *you* accountable for your parent's conduct. The Bible states: "Each of us will render an account *for himself* to God."—Romans 14:12.

● Avoid the tendency to compare yourself with other youths whose circumstances are better. (Galatians 5:26) One young man whose father abandoned his family says, "Rather than dwelling on such thoughts, it is more helpful to concentrate on ways of coping with the situation."

● Continue to show respect for a wayward parent, and if his orders don't conflict with God's standards, obey them. Jehovah's command that children honor their parents isn't dependent on whether the parent is a believer. (Ephesians 6:1-3) When you honor and obey your parents despite their failings, you prove your love for Jehovah. —1 John 5:3.

● Associate closely with the Christian congregation. There you can find the comfort of a large spiritual family. (Mark 10:30) A young man named David feared that members of the congregation might avoid him and others in his family because his father had stopped serving Jehovah. But David found that his fears were unjustified. "We weren't made to feel like outcasts," he says. "This convinced me that the congregation really cared."

**24**

# What should I do if my parents argue?

*Do your parents ever argue in front of you? If so, which of the following issues do they fight about most?*

- ☐ Money
- ☐ Household chores
- ☐ Relatives
- ☐ You

*What do you wish you could tell your parents about how this affects you? Write your comments below.*

...................................................................................

...................................................................................

YOU can't help but be affected by your parents' disputes. After all, you love them, and you rely on them for support. As a result, it may devastate you to hear them argue. You might agree with a girl named Marie, who says, "It's hard for me to respect my parents when it seems that they don't respect each other."

Seeing your parents quarrel brings home a painful realization: They aren't nearly as perfect as you might have thought. This rude awakening can arouse all kinds of fears. If the arguments are frequent or intense, you may worry that their marriage is on the verge of a breakup. "When I hear my parents fighting," says Marie, "I imagine that they'll get a divorce and that I'll have to choose which one to live with. I'm also afraid that I'll be separated from my siblings."

Why do parents fight, and what should you do when a family feud erupts?

## Why Parents Fight

As a rule, your parents may 'put up with each other in love.' (Ephesians 4:2) But the Bible says: "All have sinned and fall short of the glory of God." (Romans 3:23) Your parents aren't perfect. Therefore, it shouldn't surprise you if their irritations build and occasionally become manifest in the form of an argument.

Remember, too, that we live in "critical times hard to deal with." (2 Timothy 3:1) The pressures of making a living, paying the bills, contending with the atmosphere of the workplace—all these things place heavy strains on a marriage. And if *both* parents have secular jobs, deciding who will

**?** DID YOU KNOW . . .

People who love each other may still disagree at times.

> *Realizing that my parents aren't perfect and that they have trials just as I do has helped me to cope when they argue.* —*Kathy*

handle certain household chores can become a source of controversy.

Be assured that if your parents have disagreements, this doesn't automatically mean that their marriage is falling apart. In all likelihood your parents still love each other —even though they differ in opinion on certain matters.

To illustrate: Have you ever watched a movie with close friends and found out that your opinion of it differed from theirs? It can happen. Even people who are close to one another will see certain things differently. It could be similar with your parents. Perhaps both are concerned about the family finances, but each has a different view of budgeting; both want to plan a family vacation, but each has a different notion of what constitutes relaxation; or both are eager for you to succeed at school, but each has a different idea about the best way to motivate you.

The point is, unity does not require uniformity. Two people who love each other can see things differently at times. Still, your parents' conflicts may be difficult to listen to. What can you do or say that will help you to endure?

## What to Do

**Be respectful.** It's easy to become annoyed with bickering parents. After all, they're supposed to set the example for you—not the other way around. Treating a parent contemptuously, though, will only add to family tensions. More important, Jehovah God commands you to respect

**TIP**

If your parents' fights are frequent and intense, respectfully suggest that they seek help.

and obey your parents—even when it's not easy for you to do so.—Exodus 20:12; Proverbs 30:17.

But what if an issue your parents disagree on directly involves you? For example, suppose one of your parents is a Christian and the other is an unbeliever. Religious difficulties may arise in which you must take a stand for righteousness along with the God-fearing parent. (Matthew 10:34-37) Always do so "with a mild temper and deep respect." Your example in this regard may one day help to win over your unbelieving parent.—1 Peter 3:15.

**Remain neutral.** What can you do if your parents pressure you to take sides on issues that don't directly involve you? Strive to remain neutral. Perhaps you can excuse yourself graciously by saying something like this: "Mom and Dad, I love you both. But please don't ask me to take sides. This is something you have to work out between yourselves."

**Communicate.** Let your parents know how their quarreling makes you feel. Choose a time when you think they'll be receptive and then respectfully tell them how their fighting upsets, angers, or even frightens you. —Proverbs 15:23; Colossians 4:6.

## What Not to Do

**Don't play marriage counselor.** As a youth, you're simply not qualified to solve your parents' disputes. To illustrate: Imagine you were a passenger in a small plane and heard the pilot and the copilot arguing. Understandably, you'd be upset. But what would happen if you presumed to tell the pilots how to fly the plane or even tried to take over the controls?

Similarly, trying to 'take over the controls' by involving yourself in your parents' marital troubles would likely just make things worse. The Bible says: "By presumptuousness one only causes a struggle, but with those consulting together there is wisdom." (Proverbs 13:10) Likely your

*A youth who tells his parents how to solve their disputes is like a passenger who tells the pilots how to fly a plane*

parents can better work out their difficulties by consulting together privately.—Proverbs 25:9.

**Don't join in.** Two clashing voices are bad enough. Why add a third voice to the clamor? No matter how tempting it may be for you to join in, the fact is that it's your parents' responsibility—not yours—to resolve their disputes. Strive, then, to follow the Bible's advice to "mind your own business" in such personal matters. (1 Thessalonians 4:11) Refuse to jump into the fray.

**Don't play one parent against the other.** Some youths actually encourage their parents to argue by pitting one against the other. When Mom says no, they play on Dad's emotions and try to squeeze a yes out of him. Clever manipulation might gain you a little freedom, but in the long run, it only prolongs family strife.

**Don't let *their* behavior affect *your* behavior.** A youth named Peter came to realize that he was using unchristian conduct as a way to get back at his abusive dad. "I wanted

## >>> action plan!

*When my parents start to argue, I will*

✎ ..............................................................................................

..............................................................................................

*If my parents ask me to take sides, I will say*

..............................................................................................

..............................................................................................

*What I would like to ask my parent(s) about this subject is*

..............................................................................................

..............................................................................................

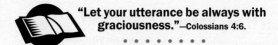

**"Let your utterance be always with graciousness."**—Colossians 4:6.

• • • • • • • • •

to hurt him," Peter says. "I resented him so much for the way he treated my mom and me and my sister." Before long, though, Peter had to face the consequences of his actions. The lesson? Bad behavior will only compound the problems you're facing at home.—Galatians 6:7.

Write here which of the points in this chapter you need to work on most. ✎ ..............................................................

Clearly, you can't stop your parents from arguing. But be assured that Jehovah can help you to cope with the anxiety that their fighting causes in you.—Philippians 4: 6, 7; 1 Peter 5:7.

Try your best to apply the above suggestions. In time, your parents may be moved to give serious attention to working out their problems. Who knows—they may even stop their fighting.

**IN OUR NEXT CHAPTER** *How can you deal with the challenges of being raised in a single-parent family?*

---

**WHAT DO YOU THINK?**

- Why do some parents fight?

- Why are you not to blame for your parents' problems?

- What can you learn from observing your parents' conduct?

# ⟫ what if my parents separate?

If your parents separate, how can you act wisely despite the feelings that may be tearing you up inside? Consider the following suggestions:

● **Resist false expectations.** Your first instinct might be to try to get your parents back together. Recalls Anne: "After they separated, my parents would still take us out together sometimes. My sister and I would whisper to each other, 'Let's run ahead and leave those two together.' But I guess it didn't work. They never did get back together."

Proverbs 13:12 says: "Expectation postponed is making the heart sick." To avoid becoming unduly distressed yourself, remember that you cannot control what your parents do. You didn't cause their separation, and in all likelihood you cannot step in and patch up their marriage either.—Proverbs 26:17.

● **Avoid hatred.** Harboring anger and hatred toward one or both of your parents can cause you long-term damage. Tom recalls his feelings at age 12: "I started to feel real anger toward my dad. I don't like to use the word 'hatred,' but I had a terrible grudge. I couldn't see how he could care about us if he left us."

Separation, though, is rarely as simple as one parent being all good and the other being all bad. The fact is, your parents probably haven't told you everything about their marriage or its breakup; they may not even understand it themselves. So avoid judging a situation when you don't have the whole picture. (Proverbs 18:13) Granted, anger is hard to resist, and it's quite natural for you to feel deeply upset for a time. But nursing an angry and vengeful spirit can gradually poison your personality. For good reason the

Bible tells us: "Let anger alone and leave rage."—Psalm 37:8.

● *Be realistic.* Rather than hate an estranged parent, some youths swing to the other extreme and idolize him or her. One youth's father, for example, was an alcoholic and a womanizer who left the family repeatedly and finally got a divorce. Yet, this youth recalls that for some reason, he almost worshipped his dad!

Such misguided adoration isn't unusual. In one country, some 90 percent of the children of divorced parents live with their mother and visit their father. Thus, the mother is often responsible for the day-to-day care of her children—including discipline. And in spite of support payments, the mother's economic status usually goes way down after the divorce. On the other hand, the father's may go *up.* The result: A visit with Dad means getting gifts and having fun! Life with Mom means pinching pennies and being told what to do and what not to do. Sad to say, some youths have even left a Christian parent in order to live with a wealthier and more permissive unbelieving parent. —Proverbs 19:4.

If you're tempted to make such a choice, check your priorities. Remember that you need moral guidance and discipline. Nothing else a parent can offer will so deeply affect your character and the quality of your life. —Proverbs 4:13.

# 25

# Can I be happy in a single-parent family?

*"Kids with two parents can have their own rooms and buy new clothes. But I have to share a room; I hardly ever get the kind of clothes I like. Mom says she can't afford them. With all the chores I have to do around the house while she works, I feel like a maid —like I'm being cheated out of part of my childhood."*—Shalonda, 13.

NO DOUBT about it, a home with two loving parents is the ideal. A dad and mom who are together can usually offer more guidance, protection, and support. "Two are better off than one," says the Bible, "because together they can work more effectively."—Ecclesiastes 4:9, *Today's English Version.*

Even so, if the two-parent home were an animal, it would likely be placed on the endangered species list. For example, more than half the children in the United States will spend some time in a single-parent family before they turn 18.

Still, some youths who live in one-parent households feel ashamed of their circumstances. Others feel overwhelmed by the pressures and problems to which life subjects them. If you live in a one-parent family, what pressures do you encounter? On the line below, write down the problem that bothers you most.

*Mom always works*

Because you're missing the full-time love and care of one of your parents, are you doomed to misery? Not at all! Much has to do with your view of the situation. Proverbs 15:15 says: "All the days of the afflicted one are bad; but the one that is good at heart has a feast constantly." As this proverb implies, a person's mood is often determined more by his attitude than by his circumstances. What can you do to help yourself feel "good at heart" despite your circumstances?

**Counteract Negative Feelings**

First, try not to allow the negative comments of others to arouse bad feelings. Some teachers, for example, have shown glaring insensitivity toward one-parent students. Some have even assumed that any behavioral problem is the result of a faulty home environment. But ask yourself: 'Do the people who make these comments really know me and my family? Or are they just parroting what they've heard others say about one-parent households?"

It's worth noting that the expression "fatherless boy" appears dozens of times in the Scriptures. Not once is this term used in a derogatory manner. In fact, in nearly every one of these accounts, Jehovah reveals his special concern for children who are raised in one-parent homes.*

On the other hand, some well-meaning people might be overly sensitive when speaking to you. For example, they may hesitate to use such words as "father," "marriage," "divorce," or "death," fearing that such words will offend or embarrass you. Does this kind of behavior bother you? If so, tactfully show them that their concerns are misplaced. Tony, 14, never knew his real father. He says some people bite their tongue when it comes to certain words. However, Tony goes right ahead and uses those very words when talking to them. "I want them to know I'm not ashamed of my situation," he says.

## Avoid the "What-Ifs"

Granted, sadness and a sense of loss are only natural if your parents have divorced or if a beloved parent has died. Even so, eventually you need to accept your situation. The Bible offers this advice: "Do not say: 'Why has it happened that the former days proved to be better than these?'" (Ecclesiastes 7:10) In this regard, 13-year-old Sarah, whose parents were divorced when she

**? DID YOU KNOW...**

Taking on responsibilities in the home can help you mature faster than youths in two-parent families, who often have less responsibility.

---

* See, for example, Deuteronomy 24:19-21 and Psalm 68:5.

was 10, recommends: "Do not brood over your situation, having the 'what-if' blues, or feel that the problems you have are because of your one-parent home, or even that kids in two-parent homes have a cushy life." This is good advice. After all, even the "ideal" family is hardly devoid of problems.

Why not picture your family as a team of oarsmen in a rowboat? Ideally, the boat would have a full crew. In a single-parent household, one of the crew is missing and the rest of the team has to work a bit harder. Does this mean that the family is a failure? No! As long as the rest of the team pull together, the boat will stay afloat and reach its destination.

## Are You Pulling Your Weight?

What specifically can you do to ensure that, along with the rest of your family, you're pulling your weight?

*A single-parent family is like a rowboat with a missing crew member —the rest of the team will have to work a bit harder, but they can succeed if they pull together*

Consider the following three suggestions:

**Learn to be frugal.** Money is a big concern in most one-parent families. What can you do to help? Tony, mentioned earlier, says: "Kids in my school demand that their parents buy them designer sneakers and clothes. They refuse to go to school without them. I don't have the latest designer clothes, but I'm neat and clean, and I take care of what I have. My mom's doing the best she can; I don't want to make it harder for her." With a little effort, you can imitate the apostle Paul, who said: "I have learned to be satisfied with what I have . . . , so that anywhere, at any time, I am content."—Philippians 4:11, 12, *TEV*.

Another way to be frugal is to avoid waste. (John 6:12) Young Rodney says: "Around the house, I try to be careful not to break or misplace things, since it costs money to repair or replace items. I try to turn off electrical appliances or lights not being used. This helps to lower our electric bills."

**Take the initiative.** Many single parents are reluctant to enforce household rules or to ask their children to help with chores. Why? Some feel that they need to compensate for the absence of a parent by making life easy for their children. 'I don't want my kids to miss out on having fun,' they may reason.

**READ MORE ABOUT THIS TOPIC IN VOLUME 1, CHAPTER 4**

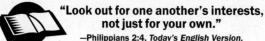

**"Look out for one another's interests,
not just for your own."**
—Philippians 2:4, *Today's English Version.*

• • • • • • • •

Now, you might be tempted to take advantage of your parent's feelings of guilt. But doing so would only add to your parent's burden, not lighten it. Instead, why not take the initiative to help out? Consider what Tony was willing to do. "My mother works in a hospital, and her uniform has to be pressed," he says. "So I iron it for her." Isn't that a woman's work? "Some think so," replies Tony. "But it helps my mom, so I do it."

**Express appreciation.** Besides offering practical help, you can do much to lift your parent's spirits by simply expressing your appreciation. One single parent wrote: "I often find that when I am really low or irritable from a particularly trying day at work and I come home—that is the

## ⟫⟫ *action plan!*

*I will counteract my negative feelings by*

✎ ....................................................................

....................................................................

*If people are overly sensitive around me,
I will say*

....................................................................

....................................................................

*What I would like to ask my parent about this
subject is*

....................................................................

....................................................................

day my daughter has chosen to set the table and get the supper going." She adds: "My son puts his arms around me and hugs me." How is she affected by such thoughtful acts? "My whole mood changes for the better again," she says.

Write here which one of the above three points you need to work on most. ✎ ....... *helping out* .........

Living in a one-parent family gives you the opportunity to develop such qualities as compassion, unselfishness, and dependability. In addition, Jesus said: "There is more happiness in giving than there is in receiving." (Acts 20:35) And great happiness can be yours if you give of yourself by helping your single parent.

Of course, you'll wish from time to time that you had a second parent at home. Still, you *can* learn to make the best of your situation. That's what a girl named Nia found. "After my dad died," she says, "someone told me that 'your life is what you make it,' and those words really stuck with me. They reminded me that I don't *have* to be a victim of my circumstances." You can adopt a similar outlook. Remember, it's not your circumstances that make you happy or unhappy. It's how you view them—and what you do about them.

**WHAT DO YOU THINK?**

- Why do some people display prejudice toward children of single parents?

- Why might your parent be reluctant to ask you to help with chores?

- How can you express appreciation for your parent?

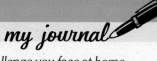
*my journal*

*Write about the most difficult challenge you face at home and why you find it so hard to deal with.*

✎

_____

_____

_____

_____

_____

_____

*After reading this section, how do you plan to cope with the problem you just wrote about?*

_____

_____

_____

_____

_____

_____

_____

_____

# 7 YOUR FEELINGS

*Which of the following statements best describes you?*

- ❏ I have problems controlling my temper.
- ❏ I'm a total failure—I can't do anything right.
- ❏ I'm always sad. There's no joy in my life.
- ❏ I just can't keep my mind off the opposite sex.
- ❏ I sometimes feel attracted to the same sex.

If you selected any of the above statements, don't despair! **Chapters 26-29** will help you learn how to control your feelings so that your feelings do not control you.

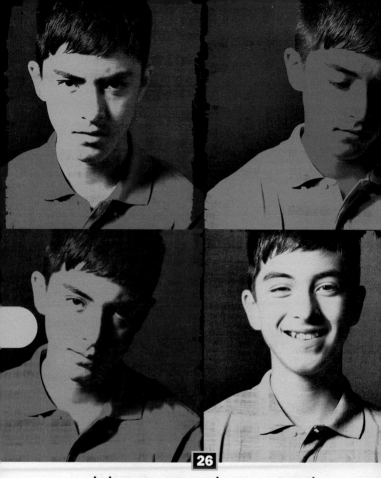

**26**

# How can I control my emotions?

WHAT do you think—is fire good or bad? You probably would say that the answer depends on the circumstances. On a cold winter night, logs burning in a fireplace can provide much-needed warmth. That's good. Uncontrolled, however, the flames can quickly spread and destroy the entire house. That's bad.

It's similar with your emotions. When controlled, they're beneficial, enabling you to develop warm friendships. Unrestrained, your emotions can be destructive, not only to you but also to those around you.

As an adolescent, you may at times find yourself overwhelmed by anger or sadness. How can you control those emotions? Let's discuss them one at a time.

## Defusing Anger

It isn't easy to deal with the hurt and pain that arise when you're a victim of mistreatment. Some in that position lose their self-control. In fact, the Bible speaks of people who are "given to anger" and "disposed to rage." (Proverbs 22:24; 29:22) This is no trivial matter. Uncontrolled anger can cause you to take action that you'll later regret. So how can you control your emotions when you've been mistreated?

First, analyze the situation squarely, and see if you can settle the matter in your heart.* (Psalm 4:4) Remember, paying back "injury for injury" will just make matters worse. (1 Thessalonians 5:15)

---

* If the mistreatment involves bullying, see Chapter 14 of this book for suggestions on how to deal with the situation. On the other hand, if a friend has made you angry, you may find the information in Chapter 10 helpful.

**DID YOU KNOW...** ❓

**When your body is deprived of sufficient rest and nutrition, you're less capable of dealing with your feelings.**

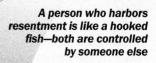

*A person who harbors resentment is like a hooked fish—both are controlled by someone else*

After thinking the matter over and praying about it, you might find that you're able to let go of resentment. Once you do that, you will reduce its hold on you. —Psalm 37:8.

But what if the hurt just won't go away? The Bible says that there is "a time to keep quiet and a time to speak." (Ecclesiastes 3:7) Can you approach the person who hurt you? If that's not advisable, you might benefit by talking to your parents or a mature friend about how you feel. If someone is purposely trying to harass you, make a special effort to be kind to that one. The chart on page 221 can help you to think up additional responses to situations that until now may have made you react impulsively.

By all means, pray to Jehovah, and ask him to help you avoid building up resentment toward the individual who hurt you. Remember this: Although you can't change what happened, you *can* change your reaction to what happened. If you let yourself be consumed with resentment, you become as helpless as a hooked fish. You allow someone else to lead your thinking and emotions. Wouldn't *you* rather be the one who is in control?—Romans 12:19.

## ✂ control your anger

| event 😕 | impulsive reaction 😠 | better response 😊 Complete the chart |
|---|---|---|
| A classmate ridicules me | Respond with an insult | Ignore the remark, and show my classmate that he will not provoke me |
| My sister "borrowed" my favorite shoes without asking me | Retaliate by "borrowing" something of hers | 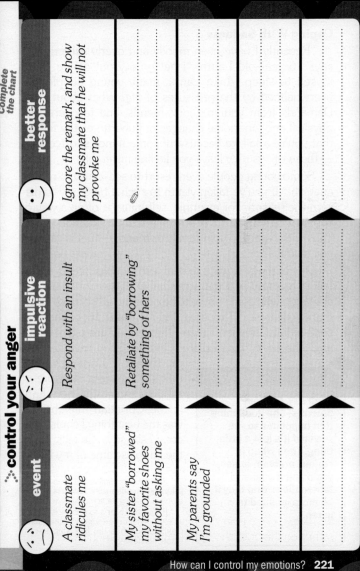 |
| My parents say I'm grounded | | |
| | | |
| | | |

## Coping With Sadness

"Recently I have been moody and overly self-critical," says 16-year-old Laura. "I get no joy out of life. I cry myself to sleep." Like Laura, many young people feel overwhelmed by the pressures of life. What about you? Demands from your parents, friends, and teachers; the physical and emotional changes of puberty; or the feeling that you're a failure because of some minor shortcoming —these things may leave you feeling miserable.

Some young people even resort to self-injury to relieve anguish.* If you've fallen victim to such a habit, try to discern the reason. For example, self-injury is often a way of coping with some form of stress. Is there a situation—perhaps with regard to your family or friends—that is causing you distress?

One of the best ways to deal with troubled feelings is to talk to a parent or a mature member of the Christian congregation who could prove to be one who is "born for when there is distress." (Proverbs 17:17) Liliana, 16, confided in some adult Christian sisters. "Since they are older than I am," she says, "their advice is sound. They have become my friends."# Dana, 15, says that she gained a measure of relief by increasing her share in the Christian ministry. "It was the best thing I could have done," she says. "In fact, it was the happiest time of my life!"

✔ **TIP**

Each day, tell your parent(s) one good thing that happened to you —even if it's just a little thing. Then when a serious problem arises, you'll find it easier to talk to them. And they'll be more inclined to listen.

---

\* Self-injurers deliberately hurt themselves by various means, such as cutting, burning, bruising, or scraping their skin.

\# If you can't bear a face-to-face talk, try writing a letter or speaking over the phone. Confiding is often the first step toward emotional healing.

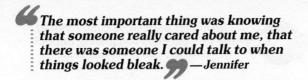

**The most important thing was knowing that someone really cared about me, that there was someone I could talk to when things looked bleak.** *—Jennifer*

Above all, if you're sad and depressed, don't neglect prayer. The psalmist David, who was no stranger to adversity, wrote: "Throw your burden upon Jehovah himself, and he himself will sustain you." (Psalm 55:22) Jehovah knows about your suffering. More than that, "he cares for you." (1 Peter 5:7) If your heart condemns you, remember that 'God is greater than your heart and knows all things.' (1 John 3:20) He understands even better than you do *why* you're distressed, and he can lift your emotional burdens.

If sadness persists, it could be that you suffer from a health disorder, such as depression.* If that's the case, it

---

* For more information on depression, see Volume 1, chapter 13.

## ⟫⟫ action plan!

*The negative emotion I contend with most is*

✎ ...................................................................................

...................................................................................

*I will deal with this negative emotion by*

...................................................................................

...................................................................................

*What I would like to ask my parent(s) about this subject is*

...................................................................................

...................................................................................

**"Do not let yourself be conquered by the evil, but keep conquering the evil with the good."**—Romans 12:21.

• • • • • • • •

would be good for you to get a medical checkup. Ignoring the situation would be like turning up the volume of a car radio to drown out a knocking noise in the engine. It's far better to address the matter. Really, there's no need to be ashamed of your condition. Many youths who suffer from depression and related disorders are being helped through treatment.

Remember, your emotions are like fire. When controlled, they're beneficial; when unrestrained, they're destructive. Do your best to keep your emotions in check. True, on occasion you will likely say or do things that you later regret. But be patient. In time, you'll learn to control your emotions so that your emotions do not control you.

**IN OUR NEXT CHAPTER** *Are you a perfectionist? If so, how can you learn to cope with your failings?*

**WHAT DO YOU THINK?**

- Why is uncontrolled anger displeasing to God?

- In what ways can having an angry disposition hurt you?

- What are some ways you can cope with sadness?

# 27

# Why do I feel that I have to be perfect?

*Do you become upset if you get anything less than a perfect score on a test?*  ❑ Yes  ❑ No

*Do you feel like a complete failure when you receive any type of criticism?*  ❑ Yes  ❑ No

*Do you find it hard to make or keep friends because no one seems to measure up to your standards?*  ❑ Yes  ❑ No

IF YOU answered yes to one or more of the above questions, you may have a problem with perfectionism. 'But what's wrong with trying to do things just right?' you might ask. Nothing, of course. The Bible praises the man who is "skillful in his work." (Proverbs 22:29) The perfectionist, however, takes things to an extreme.

For example, 19-year-old Jason admits: "During my last

**DID YOU KNOW...** ❓

Jehovah is perfect, but when dealing with imperfect humans, he is not a perfectionist. He is neither unreasonable nor unrealistic in what he expects of us.

> **Doing your best and being a perfectionist are two different things; one is balanced and the other is not.** —Megan

year of school, I felt that if I didn't get a perfect score on my tests, I wasn't a good student at all. I also play piano, and I used to feel that I had to perform with the skill of a concert pianist."

Perfectionism might even impede a person's worship. Consider what can happen to a youth who is constantly held up as an example to others. Always in the limelight, he may feel as though he's walking a tightrope, with everyone scrutinizing his performance. Of course, Christians young and old benefit from good examples in the congregation. Yet, the quest to maintain a perfect image may cause a youth to lose his joy in God's service. If that happens, the youth needs help. But he might not ask for it, fearing that he'll disappoint those who think so highly of him. He might even be tempted to give up completely, reasoning, 'If I can't live up to the perfect ideal, why try at all?'

## Battling Perfectionism

Perfectionists labor under the illusion that mistakes should never be made. Really, though, that viewpoint is flawed. The Bible plainly states: "All have sinned and fall short of the glory of God." (Romans 3:23) It's impossible, then, for any of us to be perfect in the absolute sense. In fact, believing that you can do things perfectly is as

**TIP**

Think of a task that you've held off from performing, simply because you were afraid of not doing it perfectly. Then set a date to complete it.

ROLE MODEL

# Paul

The apostle Paul is **realistic** about his feelings. He candidly admits: "When I **wish to do what is right,** what is bad is present with me." Paul is a good person at heart. "I really delight in the law of God according to the man I am within," he writes. What's the problem then? Paul says: "I behold . . . **another law** warring against the law of my mind and **leading me captive** to sin's law that is in my members." Paul's failings don't make him happy. **"Miserable** man that I am!" he exclaims.—Romans 7: 21-24.

Do your mistakes cause you to feel miserable? If so, remember that even Paul felt that way at times. But Paul also knew that Christ died for people like him, leading him to exclaim: **"Thanks to God through Jesus Christ** our Lord!" (Romans 7:25) Paul viewed the ransom as a personal gift. He wrote: "The Son of God . . . loved *me* and handed himself over for *me.*" (Galatians 2:20) When you feel down, **reflect on the ransom.** And if your failings discourage you, never forget that Christ died for sinners, not for perfect people.

## ⫶ perfectionism and friendships

**Have you shut people out of your life because they just aren't good enough for you? Or have good people stayed away from you because your standards for friendship appear to be too high? The Bible advises us: "Do not become righteous overmuch, nor show yourself excessively wise. Why should you cause desolation to yourself?" (Ecclesiastes 7:16) One way that the perfectionist causes desolation to himself is by alienating those who might otherwise enjoy his company. "No one likes to be around people who make them feel bad," says a girl named Amber, "and I've seen perfectionists lose good friends over some very small things."**

absurd as thinking that you can leap off the ground and fly. No matter how firmly you believe this, it's just *not* going to happen!

How can you keep a perfectionist mind-set from taking over your life? Try the following:

**Redefine "success."** Are you wearing yourself out trying to be the very best? The Bible indicates that such an effort can prove to be like "chasing the wind." (Ecclesiastes 4:4, *Today's English Version*) The fact is, few people ever succeed at being *"the best."* And even when a person does, it's usually just a matter of time before someone comes along who performs better. Success means doing *your* best—not outdoing *someone else's.*—Galatians 6:4.

**Be realistic.** Your expectations should be equal to your abilities *and* limitations. Setting the bar too high for yourself can be a sign of immodesty—even egotism.

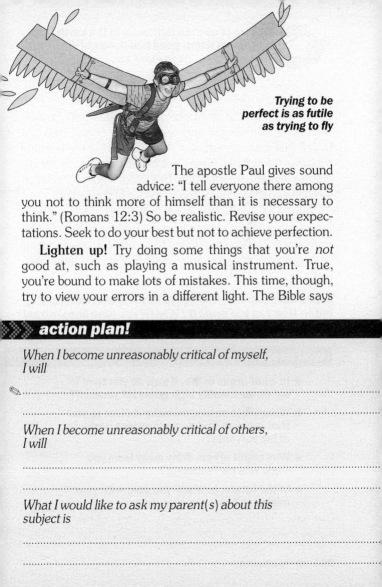

*Trying to be perfect is as futile as trying to fly*

The apostle Paul gives sound advice: "I tell everyone there among you not to think more of himself than it is necessary to think." (Romans 12:3) So be realistic. Revise your expectations. Seek to do your best but not to achieve perfection.

**Lighten up!** Try doing some things that you're *not* good at, such as playing a musical instrument. True, you're bound to make lots of mistakes. This time, though, try to view your errors in a different light. The Bible says

## ⟩⟩⟩ action plan!

*When I become unreasonably critical of myself, I will*

✎ ................................................................................

................................................................................

*When I become unreasonably critical of others, I will*

................................................................................

................................................................................

*What I would like to ask my parent(s) about this subject is*

................................................................................

................................................................................

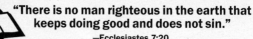

**"There is no man righteous in the earth that keeps doing good and does not sin."**
—Ecclesiastes 7:20.

• • • • • • • •

that there's "a time to laugh." (Ecclesiastes 3:4) So why not take a lighthearted approach? Doing so will help you to see that making mistakes is simply part of the learning process. Admittedly, it may not be easy for you to handle doing a less-than-perfect job. But make a conscious effort to push negative, critical thoughts out of your mind.

Always remember that Jehovah doesn't demand perfection; he simply expects us to be faithful to him. (1 Corinthians 4:2) If you're striving to be faithful, you can truly be happy with who you are—even though you aren't perfect.

**IN OUR NEXT CHAPTER** *Homosexuality is widely accepted today. How can you avoid it? What if you have homosexual desires?*

**WHAT DO YOU THINK?**

- In what areas of life, if any, do you tend to set unreasonably high goals for yourself?

- What Bible passages make it clear to you that Jehovah God doesn't expect perfection of his servants?

- Why might others draw away from you if you're a perfectionist?

- In the future, how will you deal with your mistakes?

# 28

# How can I avoid homosexuality?

*"During my teens I struggled with an attraction to other males. Deep down, I knew those thoughts weren't normal."*—Olef.

*"My girlfriend and I kissed once or twice. Since I still liked boys, I wondered if I might be bisexual."*—Sarah.

FEW would deny that homosexuality is talked about more openly today than it was several decades ago. And just try to say that you disapprove of it! Likely, you will be bombarded with criticism. Says 16-year-old Amy, "One girl told me that I must be prejudiced against people of other races, because my opinion of homosexuality amounted to the same thing—prejudice!"

Today's permissive attitudes have prompted a number of youths to experiment with same-sex relationships. "Many girls in my school claim to be either lesbian, bisexual, or 'bi-curious,'" says 15-year-old Becky. Christa, 18, finds the situation similar at her school. "Two classmates have actually propositioned me," she says. "One wrote me a note asking if I wanted to see what it was like to be with a girl."

With same-sex relationships being touted so openly, you may begin to wonder: 'Is homosexuality really that bad? What if I'm attracted to someone of my sex? Does that mean I'm gay?'

## How Does God View Homosexuality?

Today, many people—even some clergymen—soft-pedal the issue of homosexuality. Yet, God's Word, the Bible, leaves no room for confusion. It tells us that Jehovah God made man and woman and that he purposed for sexual desires to be fulfilled only between a husband and a wife. (Genesis 1:27, 28; 2:24) It comes as no surprise, then, that the Bible condemns homosexual acts. —Romans 1:26, 27.

Some would say that God's Word is out-of-date. But why, do you think, are they so quick to make that claim? Could it be because the Bible's view conflicts with their own? Many reject God's Word simply because it teaches something different from what they *want* to believe. That view is biased, though, and we should rise above such closed-minded thinking!

But what if you feel attracted to a member of the same sex? Does this automatically mean that you're a homosexual? No. Remember, you're in "the bloom of youth," a period when you're subject to involuntary sexual arousal. (1 Corinthians 7:36) If at times you feel an attraction to a member of the same sex, be assured that this doesn't mean that you're gay. Such inclinations usually fade with time. Meanwhile, you must keep from getting involved in homosexual practices. How?

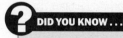

**DID YOU KNOW...**

Although you may not have complete control over your desires, you *do* have control over your actions. You can choose not to act on wrong desires.

**Pray about the matter.** Implore Jehovah as David did: "Search through me, O God, and know my heart. Examine me, and know my disquieting thoughts, and see whether there is in me any painful

*All youths face a choice—either to adopt the world's degraded view of sexuality or to follow the high moral path set forth in God's Word*

way, and lead me in the way of time indefinite." (Psalm 139: 23, 24) Jehovah can fortify you with a peace that "excels all thought." This can 'guard your heart and your mental powers' and give you "power beyond what is normal" to keep from acting on wrong desires.—Philippians 4:6, 7; 2 Corinthians 4:7.

**Fill your mind with upbuilding thoughts.** (Philippians 4:8) Read the Bible daily. Never underestimate its power to shape your mind and heart for good. (Hebrews 4:12) A young man named Jason says: "The Bible—including such scriptures as 1 Corinthians 6:9, 10 and Ephesians 5:3—has had a powerful effect on me. I read these scriptures whenever wrong desires occur."

**Shun pornography and gay propaganda.** (Colossians 3:5) Avoid anything that will arouse immoral desires. This would include pornography, certain TV shows and movies, and perhaps even fashion or bodybuilding magazines that feature lightly clad models. Change negative thoughts to positive ones. "Whenever I have homosexual urges," says one teenage boy, "I meditate on my favorite Bible text."

How can I avoid homosexuality?  **233**

**"Examine me, and know my disquieting thoughts, and see whether there is in me any painful way."**—Psalm 139:23, 24.

• • • • • • • •

Of course, some claim that there's no point in doing all this, that you should simply 'embrace your sexuality' and 'accept who you are.' But the Bible says that you can do better than that! It tells us, for example, that some early Christians who had formerly practiced homosexuality *changed.* (1 Corinthians 6:9-11) You too can win the battle—even if at this point it's only being waged in your heart.

What if same-sex desires persist? Do not give in to them! Jehovah condemns homosexual *acts.* Thus, the person who struggles with same-sex desires is presented with a reachable goal—*he or she can choose not to act on those desires.*

To illustrate: A person might be "disposed to rage." (Proverbs 29:22) In the past he may have freely given in to fits of anger. After studying the Bible, though, he becomes aware of the need to develop self-control. Does this mean that he'll never again feel anger welling up inside him? No. However, because he knows what the Bible says about uncontrolled anger, he will strive hard not to succumb to his feelings.

It's similar with a person who is attracted to others of the same sex but who has now come to learn what the

**TIP**

To develop a healthy view of masculinity, study the example of Jesus. (1 Peter 2:21) He was a perfect model of masculine power combined with gentleness.

Bible says about homosexual practices. On occasion, an improper desire may still present itself. But by viewing homosexuality the way Jehovah views it, a person can find the strength to resist that desire.

## Don't Give Up!

If you struggle with same-sex desires, you might feel as did one young man, who said: "I've tried to change my feelings. I've prayed to Jehovah for help. I read the Bible. I've heard talks on the subject. But I don't know where to turn."

If you're in a similar situation, you clearly have a real fight on your hands. There's no easy cure. Nevertheless, anyone who desires to please God must conform to His moral standards and shun immoral behavior, even though doing so may be agonizingly difficult. Never forget that God understands the struggle you have in your heart

#### ⟩⟩⟩ action plan!

*If someone asks me why the Bible condemns homosexuality, I will say*

..............................................................................

..............................................................................

*If someone says that the Bible's view is narrow-minded, I will reason with him by saying*

..............................................................................

..............................................................................

*What I would like to ask my parent(s) about this subject is*

..............................................................................

..............................................................................

> **The world's warped thinking affected my mind and added to my sexual confusion. Now I steer clear of anything or anyone that promotes homosexuality.** —Anna

and that he has compassion for those who serve him.* (1 John 3:19, 20) When you obey God's commandments, you open the way for receiving his blessing. In fact, in the keeping of God's commands, "there is a large reward." (Psalm 19:11) Even now, you'll enjoy the best way of life possible in this troubled world.

So rely on God, and fight against wrong desires. (Galatians 6:9) Strive to "abhor what is wicked" and "cling to what is good." (Romans 12:9) With time and effort, you are likely to find that the wrong desires diminish. Best of all, by avoiding homosexual practices, you'll have the prospect of living forever in God's righteous new world.

---

* A Christian who has engaged in acts of sexual misconduct should seek the help of congregation elders.—James 5:14, 15.

**IN OUR NEXT CHAPTER** *How can you control feelings of attraction to the opposite sex?*

**WHAT DO YOU THINK?**

- Why does God disapprove of homosexuality?

- What practical steps can you take to avoid being ensnared by homosexuality?

- Does adopting God's view of homosexuality mean that you're homophobic (exhibiting a hatred or strong dislike of homosexuals)?

**29**

# How can I keep my mind off sex?

"I FIND myself thinking about girls all the time—even when they're not around," says a young man named Michael. "It's ridiculous. Sometimes I can't even concentrate!"

Do you, like Michael, spend much of your waking hours daydreaming about the opposite sex? If so, you may feel that you're at war with your own brain. Thoughts about sex may march into your mind like enemy soldiers. "These thoughts can consume you," says Michael. "They can make you take the long route to your car just to pass a cute girl or get you to walk down a store aisle when you don't really need to just to take a closer look at someone."

Remember, though, that sexual feelings aren't evil in themselves. After all, God created man and woman to have a strong attraction for each other, and satisfying sexual desire is proper within the marriage arrangement. While you're still single, you may experience intense sexual urges. If that happens, don't think that you're inherently bad or that you're just not cut out for moral cleanness. *You can be chaste if you choose to be!* But being successful at your endeavor will require that you keep thoughts about the opposite sex under control. How can you do that?

**?** DID YOU KNOW . . .

**What you allow your mind to dwell on can shape your personality and affect your actions.—James 1: 14, 15.**

**Examine your associates.** If your classmates start to talk about immoral sex, you might be tempted to join in —just so you don't stand out as different. Really, though, this will only make it more difficult for you to control your thoughts. What should you do

—just get up and leave? Certainly, and you need not feel awkward about doing so! Often you can find a way to leave without appearing self-righteous and inviting ridicule.

**Shun immoral entertainment.** Of course, not every movie or CD is bad. Still, much of today's entertainment is designed to arouse improper sexual feelings. The Bible's counsel? "Let us cleanse ourselves of every defilement of flesh and spirit, perfecting holiness in God's fear." (2 Corinthians 7:1) Steer clear of any entertainment that might stimulate immoral sexual desires.*

### The Problem of Masturbation

Some youths attempt to alleviate sexual arousal by means of masturbation. But serious problems can result from this. The Bible urges Christians: "Deaden, therefore, your body members that are upon the earth as respects fornication, uncleanness, sexual appetite, hurtful desire, and covetousness." (Colossians 3:5) Masturbation is the very opposite of 'deadening sexual appetite.' Indeed, it stimulates and nurtures that appetite!

---

* Recreation and entertainment are discussed in greater detail in Section 8 of this book.

*Would you allow viruses to invade your computer? Then why invite immoral thoughts into your mind?*

> **What helps me is to change the subject—get my mind off the thoughts that cause me to feel excited. I remind myself that the feelings or urges will go away in time.** —Scott

Masturbation can make you a slave to your desires. (Titus 3:3) One way you can start to conquer the habit is to *confide in someone*. A Christian who struggled with masturbation for several years comments: "How I wish I could have summoned the courage to talk to someone about it when I was a youth! Feelings of guilt plagued me for many years, and it seriously affected my relationships with others and, above all, with Jehovah."

Whom should you talk to? A parent is often the most logical choice. Or perhaps a mature member of the Christian congregation can help. You could start by saying, "I'd like to talk to you about a problem that's bothering me a lot."

André talked to a Christian elder, and he's glad he did. "As the elder listened to me, his eyes filled with tears," André says. "When I finished, he assured me of Jehovah's love for me. He told me that my problem is a common one. He promised to check on my progress and to bring me more information from Bible-study aids. Talking with him, I resolved to keep up the fight —even if further relapses occurred."

**✔ TIP**

If you've relapsed into the habit of masturbation, don't give up the fight! Analyze what led to the relapse, and try not to repeat the same pattern.

Mário decided to talk to his father, who proved to be very sympathetic and understanding. He even admitted to Mário that in his youth he himself had found it difficult to overcome the habit. "My father's honesty and sincerity encouraged me greatly," Mário says. "I reasoned that if he had been victorious, I could be too. I was so moved by my father's attitude that I broke down and cried."

Like André and Mário, you can find help in your efforts to conquer the habit of masturbation. Even if you encounter setbacks, don't give up! Be assured that you *can* win the battle.*

## Controlling Your Thoughts

The apostle Paul said: "I pummel my body and lead it as a slave." (1 Corinthians 9:27) Similarly, you may have to be strict with yourself when improper thoughts

---

* For more information on masturbation, see Volume 1, chapters 25 and 26.

### action plan!

*When I need to get my mind off the opposite sex, I will*

..............................................................................................

..............................................................................................

*If conversation with classmates becomes suggestive or lewd, I will*

..............................................................................................

..............................................................................................

*What I would like to ask my parent(s) about this subject is*

..............................................................................................

..............................................................................................

> **"Whatever virtue there is and whatever praiseworthy thing there is, continue considering these things."**
> —Philippians 4:8.

• • • • • • • •

about the opposite sex seem to invade your mind. If the thoughts persist, try some physical exercise. The Bible says: "Bodily training is beneficial for a little." (1 Timothy 4:8) A brisk walk or a few minutes of physical exercise may be all that you need to help you fight off the distracting thoughts.

Above all, don't overlook the help that is available from your heavenly Father. "When I feel sexual urges coming on," says one Christian, "I really make myself pray." No, God won't take away your interest in the opposite sex. But with his help, you can discover that there are many other things to think about.

## WHAT DO YOU THINK?

- Why should sexual feelings not always be viewed as "the enemy"?

- Why do you need to keep your sexual feelings under control?

- What types of entertainment might cause you to dwell on thoughts about the opposite sex?

- Why is it important to walk away from a conversation that has become suggestive or lewd?

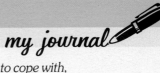

*my journal*

*What feeling do you find hardest to cope with, and how does it affect you?*

*How could you use the information in this section to help you deal with this feeling in the future?*

# RECREATION 8

*How often do you enjoy some form of recreation, such as sports, music, movies, TV, or electronic games?*

❑ Rarely
❑ Once a day
❑ Several times a day

*Who or what has the most influence on your choice of recreation?*

❑ Your peers
❑ Your parent(s)
❑ Advertising

You and your peers likely have more options for recreation than any other generation in history. But you have only a limited number of hours in a day. And the type of recreation you choose can affect your thinking and attitudes. So, what's a reasonable amount of time to devote to recreation? And how can you figure out what type to choose? **Chapters 30-33** will help you to take a serious look at how you have fun.

**30**

# Should I play electronic games?

"COMPUTER games are exciting and cool," says a boy named Brian. "You get to do things in the game that you would never actually do in real life—not without getting into serious trouble, that is." Deborah says that she too enjoys playing computer games. However, she adds a word of caution: "They can be very time-consuming, almost addictive."

Without a doubt, electronic games are more than just high-tech entertainment. Sure, they challenge your skill and help keep boredom at bay. But they do more. Electronic games can sharpen your reflexes. Some of them may even enhance your math and reading skills. Besides, the latest electronic game is likely to be the basis for school-yard conversation. If you've played the game, you have something to talk about with your peers.

Certainly, if you choose carefully, you should be able to find a game that is both exciting and acceptable. Why, though, do you need to be cautious?

## Their Dark Side

Unfortunately, not all electronic games are harmless fun. A lot of today's entertainment software enthusiastically promotes what the Bible calls "works of the flesh"—unclean practices that God condemns.—Galatians 5:19-21.

Adrian, 18, describes one best-selling game as featuring "gang wars, drug use, explicit sexual content, foul language, intense violence, blood, and gore." Some games glorify occult practices. And each new

**DID YOU KNOW...** ?

The world's first rehabilitation clinic caring exclusively for addicts of online games was opened in Amsterdam, Netherlands, in 2006.

release seems to make previous games look tame in comparison. Many of these violent games can be played live on the Internet. That ability takes gaming to a whole new level. "From your home computer," says 19-year-old James, "you can challenge people who live on the other side of the world."

Internet role-playing games have become hugely popular. In these, participants create online characters —whether human, animal, or a blend of both—that inhabit a computer-generated world populated by thousands of other players. This online world contains shops, cars, homes, dance clubs, brothels—in many ways, it is a replica of the real world. The players in these games are able to instant message each other as their computer-generated characters, called avatars, interact.

Mafia men, pimps, prostitutes, extortionists, counterfeiters, and assassins are just a few of the sordid characters that inhabit these online worlds. Players can indulge in activities they would never carry out in real life. Just by pressing a few buttons, avatars can engage in sex while the real-world participants talk about sex via instant messaging. Some games enable players' avatars to have sex with avatars that resemble children. Critics are understandably concerned that people would make a game out of such perverse acts.

## Why Your Choice Matters

Those who play these violent or sexually graphic games may say:

> *Many games desensitize you to things like violence, foul language, and immorality and can cause you to let down your guard in other aspects of life. You have to be very careful what you choose to play.* —Amy

"No harm done. It's not real. It's just a game." But don't be fooled by such false reasoning!

The Bible says: "Even by his practices a boy makes himself recognized as to whether his activity is pure and upright." (Proverbs 20:11) If you play violent, immoral games, could you be described as being pure and upright? Studies repeatedly show that watching violent entertainment increases aggression in those who view it. In fact, some experts say that because of the interactive nature of electronic games, they can have a stronger effect than TV.

Choosing to play violent or immoral electronic games is like choosing to play with radioactive waste—the damaging effects may not be immediately obvious, but they're inevitable. In what way? Exposure to high doses of radiation can destroy the lining of the stomach and allow bacteria from the intestines to invade the bloodstream, resulting in sickness. Similarly, exposure to high doses of graphic sex and hideous violence can damage your "moral sense" and allow fleshly

**TIP**

Write a brief review of each of the games you want to play, outlining the goal of the game and the methods used to achieve that goal. Compare your review with the Bible principles mentioned in this chapter, and then determine if the game is suitable.

desires to invade and dominate your thinking and actions.—Ephesians 4:19; Galatians 6:7, 8.

## What Game Should I Choose?

If your parents allow you to play electronic games, how can you know which to choose and how much time to devote to them? Ask yourself the following questions:

*How will my choice affect the way Jehovah feels about me?* "Jehovah himself examines the righteous one as well as the wicked one, and anyone loving violence His soul certainly hates," states Psalm 11:5. Regarding those who engage in occult practices, God's Word says: "Everybody doing these things is something detestable to Jehovah." (Deuteronomy 18:10-12) If you want to be a friend of God, you need to follow the advice recorded at Psalm 97: 10: "Hate what is bad."

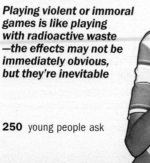

*Playing violent or immoral games is like playing with radioactive waste —the effects may not be immediately obvious, but they're inevitable*

**How will the game affect my thinking?** Ask yourself, 'Will playing this game make it easier or harder for me to "flee from fornication"?' (1 Corinthians 6:18) Games that expose you to sexually arousing images or conversations won't help you to keep your mind on things that are righteous, chaste, and virtuous.—Philippians 4:8.

**How much time will I spend playing the game?** Even the most innocent of games can consume a lot of time. So keep a log of how much time you spend gaming. Is it crowding out time you need for more important activities? Keeping track of where your time is going will help you get your priorities straight.—Ephesians 5:16.

Of course, the Bible doesn't require that you spend your whole life studying or doing chores. On the contrary, it reminds all of us that there is "a time to laugh . . . and a time to skip about." (Ecclesiastes 3:4) It's worth noting,

### action plan!

*If a friend asks me to play a violent or immoral electronic game, I will say*

✎ .............................................................................

.............................................................................

*I will limit my time playing electronic games to ...............
a week, and I can keep to this limit if I*

.............................................................................

.............................................................................

*What I would like to ask my parent(s) about this
subject is*

.............................................................................

.............................................................................

though, that the expression "to skip about" implies not only play but also physical activity. So why not use some of your free time to play games that involve physical activity instead of limiting yourself to sitting in front of a video screen?

## Choose Wisely

Without a doubt, playing electronic games can be fun, especially if you get good at it. And herein lies the very reason for you to choose your games wisely. Ask yourself, 'What subjects do I do best in at school?' Aren't they usually the ones that you enjoy? In fact, it often follows that the more you enjoy a subject, the greater the impression it makes on you. Now ask yourself: 'What game do I enjoy the most? What moral lessons is this game teaching me?'

Rather than playing a game just because your peers enjoy it, have the strength to make your own informed choice. Most important of all, apply the Bible's advice: "Keep on making sure of what is acceptable to the Lord."—Ephesians 5:10.

**IN OUR NEXT CHAPTER** *You love music, and that's normal. But are you a slave to it?*

---

**WHAT DO YOU THINK?**

- What effect can electronic games have on a person's thinking and emotions?

- Why is it important to consider Jehovah's moral standards when choosing a game?

- How would you help a younger sibling who is hooked on playing a game that you know is bad?

# 31

# How can I keep music in its place?

***How important is music to you?***
- ☐ I can live without it.
- ☐ I would die without it.

***When do you listen to music?***
- ☐ When traveling
- ☐ When studying
- ☐ All the time

***What is your favorite style of music, and why?*** ............................................

............................................

THE capacity to enjoy melody and harmony appears to be programmed into all of us. And for many youths, music is a must-have. "I can't live without it," says 21-year-old Amber. "My music is almost always playing—even when I'm cleaning, cooking, running errands, or studying."

Rhythm may be based on simple math, but music transcends cold logic and taps straight into our core emotions. Just as "a word at its right time is O how good!" a song at the right time can be so consoling! (Proverbs 15:23) "Sometimes you think that no one else understands your feelings," says 16-year-old Jessica. "But when I listen to my favorite band, I know I'm not the only one who gets depressed."

## Battleground or Common Ground?

While you no doubt love your music, your parents may have a different viewpoint. "My dad says, 'Turn off that noise! It's hurting my ears!'" comments one teenage boy. Tired of the hassle, you may feel that your parents are making a big deal out of nothing. "What about when *they* were young?" argues one teenage girl. "Didn't *their* parents think their music was bad?" Ingred, 16, complains: "Adults seem to be stuck in the past. It would be great if they recognized that our generation has some taste in music too!"

Ingred has a point. As you may know, throughout history, older and younger generations have tended to clash over matters of personal taste. But such differences don't mean that the subject

**? DID YOU KNOW...**

If you're reluctant to let your parents hear your favorite tunes, it could be a sign that something is wrong with your taste in music.

*Music is like food. The right type in the right amount is good for you. The wrong type in any amount is bad*

of music must always become a battleground. The key is to see if you can find some common ground with your parents. If your parents respect the Bible, you have a real advantage. Why? Because God's Word can help both you and your parents to discern what is definitely unacceptable and where there is room for personal taste. To do this, you need to analyze two key factors: (1) the message of the music you listen to and (2) the amount of music you listen to. First, let's consider the question . . .

## What Is the Message of My Music?

Music is like food. The right type in the right amount is good for you. The wrong type in any amount is bad. Unfortunately, with music it's the bad stuff that can be the most appealing. "Why do all the good tunes get saved for the really ugly lyrics?" laments a youth named Steve.

If you love the sound, does the message really matter? To help answer that question, ask yourself: 'If someone wanted to make me swallow poison, how would they coax me into taking it? Would they dip it in vinegar or coat it with candy?' The faithful man Job asked: "Does not the ear itself test out words as the palate tastes food?" (Job 12:11) So rather than just swallowing a song because

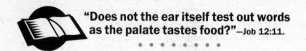

you like its beat or melody—the candy coating, so to speak—'test out the words' by considering the title and the lyrics. Why? Because the lyrics embedded in the music will affect your thinking and attitudes.

Regrettably, a great deal of today's most innovative music features lyrics that promote sex, violence, and drug abuse. If you don't feel that listening to such lyrics affects you, then you've already started to succumb to the "poison."

### Think for Yourself

Your peers may put tremendous pressure on you to listen to degrading music. There's also pressure from the music industry itself. With the help of radio, the Internet, and television, music has become a powerful, multibillion-dollar industry. High-powered marketing experts are hired to shape and control your taste in music.

But when you let your peers or the media dictate what you listen to, you lose your power of choice. You become a mindless slave. (Romans 6:16) The Bible urges you to resist the world's influence in such matters. (Romans 12:2) So you would do well to train your own "perceptive powers . . . to distinguish both right and wrong." (Hebrews 5:14)

> **TIP**
>
> If you want your parents to understand why *you* like a certain song or band, take the initiative to try to develop an appreciation for some of the music *they* enjoy.

# David

David loves music. He's a **gifted musician** and a talented songwriter. He even makes his own instruments. (2 Chronicles 7:6) David is so skilled that the king of Israel summons him to **perform in the royal court.** (1 Samuel 16:15-23) David accepts. But he **doesn't become conceited,** nor does he allow music to dominate his life. Rather, he uses his talents to praise Jehovah.

Do you love music? You may not be a talented musician, but you can still **imitate David's example.** How? By not letting music dominate your life or induce you to think and act in ways that dishonor God. Instead, use music to **enhance your enjoyment** of life. The ability to create and enjoy music is a **gift from God.** (James 1:17) David used this gift in ways that pleased Jehovah. Will you do the same?

## :» broaden your taste in music

Do you like more types of food now than you did when you were five years old? If so, that's because you have acquired a taste for new flavors. It's similar with music. Don't limit yourself to just one style. Try expanding your taste in music.

One way to do so is to learn to play an instrument. Not only can this be challenging and satisfying but it may expose you to other forms of music besides the usual commercial fodder. Where might you find the time to learn? You could buy out time from watching TV or playing electronic games. Note what these youths say.

*"Playing an instrument is a lot of fun and can be a great way to express your feelings. Learning to play new songs has taught me to like a broad range of musical styles."*
—Brian, 18, plays guitar, drums, and piano.

*"You need to practice if you want to learn to play an instrument well. And practice isn't always fun. But mastering a piece of music gives you a good feeling, a sense of accomplishment."*—Jade, 13, plays the viola.

*"When I'm having a hard day or I'm feeling down, playing my guitar really helps me to relax. It feels so good to create music that is pleasurable and soothing."*
—Vanessa, 20, plays guitar, piano, and clarinet.

*"I used to think, 'I'll never be as good as this person or that person.' But I stuck with my lessons, and now I feel real satisfaction when I play a piece of music well. I also have an increased appreciation for the skill of other musicians."*—Jacob, 20, plays guitar.

> **I sometimes catch myself listening to a song that I know isn't good for me. I turn it off immediately. If I don't, I find that I start to justify listening to it.** —Cameron

How can you use your perceptive powers when choosing music? Consider the following suggestions:

**Examine the packaging.** Often, one look at the packaging or promotional material is enough to determine the content. Violent, sexually explicit, or occult images should be a warning. The music inside is probably objectionable too.

**Check out the lyrics.** What is being said? Do you really want to listen to or repeat those ideas over and over again? Are the thoughts expressed in harmony with your values and with Christian principles?—Ephesians 5: 3-5.

**Notice the effect.** "I found that a lot of the music and lyrics I listened to made me depressed," says a youth named Philip. Granted, music may affect people in different ways. But what mood does your music nurture in you? Ask yourself: 'Do I find myself dwelling on wrong thoughts after hearing the music or the lyrics? Are slang expressions that are used in the music starting to creep into my vocabulary?'—1 Corinthians 15:33.

**Consider others.** How do your parents feel about your music? Ask them for their opinion. Think, too, of how fellow Christians might feel. Would some be disturbed by your music? The ability to modify your behavior out of respect for the feelings of others is a sign of maturity.—Romans 15:1, 2.

By asking yourself the above questions, you will be in a position to choose music that stirs your spirit without killing your spirituality. But there's one more factor to consider.

## How Much Is Too Much?

Good music, like good food, can be healthful. However, a wise proverb warns: "Is it honey that you have found? Eat what is sufficient for you, that you may not take too much of it and have to vomit it up." (Proverbs 25: 16) Honey has well-known curative properties. Yet, too much of even a *good* thing can be bad for you. The point? Good things should be enjoyed in moderation.

Some youths, however, allow music to dominate their lives. For example, Jessica, quoted earlier, confesses: "I listen to music all the time—even when I'm studying the Bible. I tell my parents that it helps me to concentrate. But they don't believe me." Does Jessica's comment sound familiar?

How can you determine how much music is too much? Ask yourself the following questions:

*How much time do I spend listening to music each day?* ✎............................................

*How much money do I spend on music each month?*

............................................

*Is my music interfering with my family relationships?* If so, write below how you might improve the situation.

.......................................................................................................

.......................................................................................................

## Modifying Your Listening Habits

If music is taking too much of a bite out of your personal life, you would do well to set limits and be more moderate in your listening habits. For example, you may need to break the habit of plugging your ears with headphones all day long or turning music on the minute you get home.

In fact, why not learn to savor some periods of silence? Doing so may help you with your studies. "You'll get a whole lot more out of them if the music is off," says Steve, quoted earlier. Try studying *without* music, and see if your concentration improves.

You will also want to schedule time for reading and studying the Bible and Bible-based publications. Jesus

## ▶▶▶ *action plan!*

*I can control my music if I*

✎ .............................................................................................

.............................................................................................

*If my peers pressure me to listen to unacceptable music, I will say*

.............................................................................................

.............................................................................................

*What I would like to ask my parent(s) about this subject is*

.............................................................................................

.............................................................................................

Christ at times sought out a quiet place for prayer and meditation. (Mark 1:35) Is your study environment similarly quiet and peaceful? If not, you may be stunting your spiritual growth.

## Make the Right Choice

Music is truly a gift from God, but you must take care not to misuse it. Don't be like the girl named Marlene who admits: "I have music that I know I'm supposed to throw out. But it sounds so good." Think of the harm that she is doing to her mind and heart by listening to what is bad! Avoid that snare. Don't let music corrupt you or take over your life. Hold to high Christian standards in choosing your music. Pray for God's guidance and help. Seek out companions who share your convictions.

Music can help you relax and unwind. It can help fill the void when you're lonely. But when the music stops, your problems are still there. And songs are no substitute for real friends. So don't allow music to become the big thing in your life. Enjoy it, but keep it in its place.

**IN OUR NEXT CHAPTER** *You need to relax once in a while. How can Bible principles help you to make the most of the good times?*

---

### WHAT DO YOU THINK?

- Why is your choice of music so important?

- How can you determine if a song is acceptable or not?

- What can you do to broaden your taste in music?

**32**

# How can I have a good time?

*Mark the following statements true or false.*
*According to the Bible . . .*

*It's always wrong to take*
*part in sports.* ❏ True ❏ False

*All movies and TV shows*
*are a bad influence.* ❏ True ❏ False

*Any sort of dancing*
*is condemned.* ❏ True ❏ False

YOU'VE worked hard all week. School is over. Your chores are completed. And you still have some energy to burn, one of the blessings of being young. (Proverbs 20:29) Now all you want to do is have some fun.

Your peers may feel that the Bible is *anti*-fun, that it restricts you from enjoying yourself. But is that true? Let's consider the true-or-false statements listed on the preceding page and see what the Bible really says about having a good time.

● **It's always wrong to take part in sports.**

**False.** The Bible says that "bodily training is beneficial." (1 Timothy 4:8) The original Greek expression for "training" that Paul used here means 'training as a gymnast' and carries the idea of exercise. Today there are numerous sports—such as skating, cycling, jogging, tennis, baseball, soccer, and volleyball, to name just a few—that can be both good exercise and fun.

Does this mean that there's no need for caution? Well, consider the context of the verse quoted above. When writing to the young man Timothy, the apostle Paul said: "Bodily training is beneficial for a little; but godly devotion is beneficial for all things, as it holds promise of the life now and that which is to come." Paul's words remind us that our first priority should always be to please God. You can ensure that godly devotion is your top priority—even when choosing a sport—by asking yourself the following three questions:

**1.** *What degree of risk is involved in the sport?* Don't simply rely on hearsay or on the enthusiastic reports of other youths. Get the facts. For example, find out the following: Just what is the accident rate for this particular

READ MORE ABOUT THIS TOPIC IN VOLUME 1, CHAPTER 37

sport? What safety precautions are taken? What training and equipment are needed to play this sport safely? While there are incidental risks in virtually any activity, is the primary objective of this sport to defy injury or death?

Life is a gift from God, and God's Law given to the Israelites imposed serious penalties if a life was taken accidentally. (Exodus 21:29; Numbers 35:22-25) God's people were thereby encouraged to be safety conscious. (Deuteronomy 22:8) Christians today likewise have an obligation to show respect for life.

**2.** *Will the sport provide good association?* If you have some athletic ability, your peers and teachers might exert pressure on you to join a school team. You may feel a strong urge to accept the offer. A Christian youth named Mark says, "I feel it's just not fair that my parents won't let me join the school team." But instead of attempting to coax your parents into accepting your viewpoint, consider the following facts: Practice sessions and games are usually scheduled outside of normal school hours. If you do well, you'll be encouraged to devote more time to the sport. If you don't do so well, you'll feel pressure to spend more

time in practice. In addition, teammates often form close bonds of friendship as they revel in the highs of victory and share the despair of defeat.

Now ask yourself: 'Will spending my personal time in an activity that could result in close bonds of friendship with youths who don't share my spiritual standards be a good influence on me?' (1 Corinthians 15:33) 'What price am I willing to pay just to play on a particular team?'

**3.** *How much time and money will the sport consume?* The Bible instructs us to "make sure of the more important things." (Philippians 1:10) To help you apply this advice, ask yourself: 'Will playing this sport eat into time that I've allocated for schoolwork or spiritual activities? What is the total monetary cost of the sport? Does my budget allow for this expense?' Answering these questions will help you to keep your priorities in order.

● *All movies and TV shows are a bad influence.*

**False.** The Bible commands Christians to "hold fast to what is fine" and to "abstain from every form of wicked-

**"Rejoice, young man, in your youth, . . . and walk in the ways of your heart and in the things seen by your eyes. But know that on account of all these the true God will bring you into judgment."**—Ecclesiastes 11:9.

• • • • • • • •

ness." (1 Thessalonians 5:21, 22) Not all movies and TV shows conflict with that standard.*

Certainly, going to a movie can be a fun way to spend time with friends. A South African girl named Leigh says, "If I'm keen on seeing a certain movie, I phone one of my friends, and we spread the word to our other friends." Usually this group attends an early showing of the movie. Afterward, their parents pick them up, and together all of them eat out.

Movies and TV may be modern inventions, but they're really just new expressions of an ancient tradition—that of storytelling. Jesus was a master at reaching peoples' hearts by means of stories. For example, his parable about the neighborly Samaritan stirs feelings of empathy and teaches profound moral lessons.—Luke 10:29-37.

Today moviemakers also teach lessons that mold people's moral perceptions. They try to make viewers identify with the characters portrayed—even when the hero is a criminal or a sadistic, power-hungry person. If you aren't careful, you may find yourself rooting for a criminal, mentally justifying his immoral or cruel acts! How can you avoid this trap?

When choosing a movie or a TV show, ask yourself: 'Will this program encourage me to be tenderly compassionate?' (Ephesians 4:32) 'Or will it coax me

---

* For more information, see Volume 1, chapter 36.

into rejoicing over another's disaster?' (Proverbs 17:5) 'Will it make it difficult for me to "hate what is bad"?' (Psalm 97:10) 'Will I, in effect, be aligning myself with "evildoers"?'—Psalm 26:4, 5.

Movie reviews and advertisements can give you some idea of the content of a movie. But don't naively put "faith in every word." (Proverbs 14:15) Why not? A movie review merely reflects another person's opinion. And an advertisement may deliberately conceal the fact that a movie has offensive scenes. A teenager named Connie says, "I've found that knowing who the principal actors are in the movie often gives you some idea of what the movie is likely to portray."

Christian peers who share your Bible-based values may know if a certain film is acceptable. But remember, people tend to tell you what they really enjoyed about a movie. Why not ask what's

*A soldier is vulnerable to an attack when his guard is down—and you are vulnerable to an attack on your morals when you're relaxing*

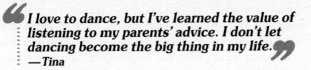

*I love to dance, but I've learned the value of listening to my parents' advice. I don't let dancing become the big thing in my life.*
—Tina

*bad* about it? Be specific. For example, inquire as to whether there are scenes of violence, sex, or demon possession. Your parents are also a good source of advice. Says young Vanessa: "I consult my parents. If they think it's all right for me to watch, I'll go see it."

Don't take the matter of choosing a movie or a TV program lightly. Why? Because the entertainment you select opens a window to your heart, revealing what values you treasure. (Luke 6:45) Your choices tell much about the kind of association you delight in, the type of language you condone, the sexual morals you tolerate. So be selective!

● *Any sort of dancing is condemned.*

**False.** When the Israelites crossed the Red Sea and escaped the Egyptian army, Miriam led the women in a celebratory dance. (Exodus 15:20) Also, in Jesus' parable of the prodigal son, the rejoicing that occurred over the son's return included "a music concert and dancing."
—Luke 15:25.

The same is true today. In many cultures dancing is enjoyed by both young and old when family and friends gather together. However, there's a need for caution. While the Bible doesn't condemn modest social gatherings, it does warn

**DID YOU KNOW...**

Dancing and music were an important part of true worship for the Israelites.—Psalm 150:4.

against "revelries," or "wild parties." (Galatians 5:19-21; *Byington*) The prophet Isaiah wrote: "Woe to those who are getting up early in the morning that they may seek just intoxicating liquor, who are lingering till late in the evening darkness so that wine itself inflames them! And there must prove to be harp and stringed instrument, tambourine and flute, and wine at their feasts; but the activity of Jehovah they do not look at."—Isaiah 5:11, 12.

Those gatherings featured the use of "intoxicating liquor" and wild music. They started early and lasted well into the evening. Note, too, the attitudes of the revelers —they behaved as if God did not exist! Little wonder, then, that God condemned such gatherings.

If you're invited to attend a party where there will be dancing, ask yourself such questions as: 'Who will be going? What kind of reputation do they have? Who is

#### ⟫⟫⟫ action plan!

*If I'm invited to join an after-school sports team, I will say*

✎

..............................................................................

..............................................................................

*If a movie that I'm watching with my friends is objectionable, I will*

..............................................................................

..............................................................................

*What I would like to ask my parent(s) about this subject is*

..............................................................................

..............................................................................

taking responsibility for the event? What supervision will there be? Do my parents approve of my attending the party? What type of dancing will be featured?' Many dance styles are designed solely to arouse sexual desire. Would engaging in or just watching such dancing help you to "flee from fornication"?—1 Corinthians 6:18.

What if you're invited to go dancing at a nightclub? Consider the comments of a youth named Shawn who before becoming a Christian would often hang out at dance clubs. He recalls: "The music is usually debasing, the dancing is usually highly immoral, and a great majority of the people who go there have a motive." That motive, says Shawn, is to leave the club with someone to have sex. After studying the Bible with Jehovah's Witnesses, Shawn had a change of heart. His opinion? "Those clubs are not the place for Christians."

## Why Stay Alert?

When do you think a soldier is more vulnerable to an attack—when he's on the battlefield or when he's relaxing with his companions? Really, it's when he's relaxing that his defenses are down and he's most vulnerable. Similarly, when you're at school or at work, your spiritual defenses are up. You're alert to possible danger. It's later when you relax with your friends that you're most vulnerable to an attack on your moral standards.

Some of your peers may ridicule you for sticking to the Bible's high moral standards when it comes to having a good time. Pressure may even come from youths who have been raised by Christian parents. But such youths have had their consciences seared. (1 Timothy 4:2) They may accuse you of being unbalanced or self-righteous. Rather than give in to peer pressure, however, "hold a good conscience."—1 Peter 3:16.

What really counts isn't what your peers think of you but what Jehovah thinks of you! And if your friends hassle you for following your conscience, it's time to find some new friends. (Proverbs 13:20) Remember, *you* are the ultimate guardian of your moral standards—even when you're having a good time.—Proverbs 4:23.

**IN OUR NEXT CHAPTER** *Pornography is more prevalent and easier to access than ever. How can you avoid this snare?*

---

### WHAT DO YOU THINK?

- **Why should Christians avoid high-risk sports?**

- **How can you determine if a movie is suitable?**

- **How would you define what is an acceptable style of dancing?**

## 33

# Why avoid pornography?

**How frequently do you come across pornography by accident?**
- ❏ Never
- ❏ Rarely
- ❏ Regularly

**Where does this most often occur?**
- ❏ Internet
- ❏ School
- ❏ TV
- ❏ Other

**How do you respond?**
- ❏ I turn away immediately.
- ❏ Curiosity causes me to look at it briefly.
- ❏ I stare at it and even search out more.

WHEN your parents were your age, people who wanted to view pornography had to search for it. Today, it seems, pornography searches for *you*. Says one 19-year-old girl, "Sometimes I'm browsing or shopping on the Internet or even just checking bank statements online when *wham*—pornography pops up!" This is hardly unusual. In one survey, 90 percent of youths between the ages of 8 and 16 said that they had unintentionally encountered pornography online—in most cases, while doing homework!

In view of its prevalence, you might wonder, 'Is pornography really all that bad?' The answer is *yes!* Pornography demeans both those who take part in it and those who look at it, and it's often a stepping-stone to committing sexual sins. But there's more.

Viewing pornography can become a habit with long-lasting, devastating effects. For example, consider a man named Jeff who even after 14 years of being free of pornography admitted: "It's a daily battle. The desire, although much more subdued, is still there. The curiosity is still there. The images are still there. I wish I'd never started down this hideous path. It seemed so harmless at first. But now I know better. Pornography is damaging, it is perverse, and it is demeaning to all parties concerned. Despite what its proponents may claim, there is nothing —absolutely nothing—positive about pornography."

**DID YOU KNOW...**

An obsession with pornography mimics the inordinate sexual fixation of the wicked spirits in Noah's day. —Genesis 6:2.

## Evaluating the Situation

How can you avoid even unintentionally stumbling across pornography? First,

> **"Deaden, therefore, your body members that are upon the earth as respects fornication, uncleanness, sexual appetite, hurtful desire, and covetousness, which is idolatry."**
> —Colossians 3:5.

• • • • • • • • •

analyze the situation. Is there a pattern to your encounters? Consider the following examples:

*Are some of your schoolmates likely to send pornography via e-mail or cell phone?* If so, it would be wise to delete their messages without opening them.

*When you're online, do pop-ups occur when you enter certain words in a search engine?* Knowing that this is possible could help you to be more specific and careful in your use of keywords.

Below, list any circumstances that have led to your encountering pornography.

.................................................................................

.................................................................................

Is there anything you can do to reduce or eliminate those accidental encounters? If so, write below what you plan to do.

.................................................................................

.................................................................................

### If You're Already Hooked

It's one thing to stumble across pornography by accident but quite another to look at it *intentionally.* What if it's even becoming a habit? Make no mistake—breaking such a habit isn't easy. To illustrate: Suppose your hands were tied together with a single cotton thread. You could

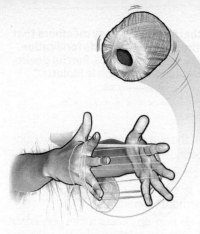

*Pornography has a cumulative effect —the more times you view it, the harder it is to break free*

probably break the thread by simply pulling your hands apart. But what if it were wrapped around your hands many times? Breaking free would be much more difficult. The same is true of people who habitually view pornography. The more they look at it, the more ensnared they become. If this has happened to you, how can you break free?

**Understand pornography for what it is.** Pornography is nothing less than a satanic attempt to degrade something that Jehovah created to be honorable. Understanding pornography in this light will help you to "hate what is bad."—Psalm 97:10.

**Consider the consequences.** Pornography destroys marriages. It devalues those depicted in it. It debases the person who views it. For good reason, the Bible

> **TIP**
>
> Make sure that your computer is set to block access to pornographic sites. Also, avoid clicking on links in unsolicited e-mails.

says: "Shrewd is the one that has seen the calamity and proceeds to conceal himself." (Proverbs 22:3) Write below one example of a calamity that could befall you if you were to view pornography habitually.

........................................................................

**Make a commitment.** "I have made a solemn promise never to look with lust at a girl," said the faithful man Job. (Job 31:1, *Today's English Version*) The following are some 'solemn promises' you could make:

*I will not use the Internet when I am alone in the room.*

*I will immediately exit any pop-up or site that is explicit.*

*I will talk to a mature friend if I have a relapse.*

Can you think of one or two other resolves that could help you in the battle against pornography? If so, list them here.........................................................................

........................................................................

........................................................................

**Pray about the matter.** The psalmist implored Jehovah: "Make my eyes pass on from seeing what is

>>> **action plan!**

*To shield myself from exposure to pornography, I will*

........................................................................

........................................................................

*What I would like to ask my parent(s) about this subject is*

........................................................................

........................................................................

> *Before studying the Bible, I had experimented heavily with nearly every major drug. But of all my addictions, pornography was by far the most difficult to break. It's only with Jehovah's help that I've been able to deal with this problem.* —Jeff

worthless." (Psalm 119:37) Jehovah God wants you to succeed, and he can give you the strength to do what is right!—Philippians 4:13.

**Talk to someone.** Choosing a confidant is often an important step in breaking the habit. (Proverbs 17:17) Write below the name of a mature person whom *you* would feel comfortable approaching about the matter.

✎ ......................................................................

Be assured that you *can* succeed in your fight to steer clear of pornography. In fact, each time you avoid it, you have won a significant victory. Tell Jehovah about that victory, and thank him for the strength he has given you. Always remember that by avoiding the plague of pornography, you make Jehovah's heart rejoice!—Proverbs 27:11.

---

**WHAT DO YOU THINK?**

- How does pornography degrade something that is honorable?

- How would you help a sibling who has a problem with pornography?

*my journal*

*Describe the type of recreation you enjoy most and why you like it so much.*

✎

_____

_____

_____

_____

_____

*Imagine that you had to explain to a younger brother or sister why it's important to keep recreation in its proper place. What would you say?*

_____

_____

_____

_____

_____

_____

# YOUR SPIRITUAL GROWTH 9

*Which of the following do you find to be most challenging?*

- ❏ Studying the Bible
- ❏ Praying regularly to Jehovah God
- ❏ Talking to others (especially my peers) about my faith
- ❏ Understanding the wisdom of Bible standards

*On the line below, write down what goal you would like to set regarding the activity that is most challenging for you.*

.................................................................................

**Chapters 34-38** will help you see how you can strengthen your spirituality, live by Bible standards, and set goals that will give your life direction and purpose.

# 34

# Why live by Bible standards?

You're in the cafeteria eating lunch with two girls at school when the new boy walks in.

"You know, Brett really likes you," the first girl says to you. "I can tell by the way he stares at you. His eyes are all over you!"

"And guess what?" the second girl whispers as she leans toward you. "He's available!"

You already suspected all of that. After all, just the other day Brett invited you to his house for a

*party. You declined, of course, although you secretly wondered what it would have been like.*

*The first girl interrupts your thoughts.*

*"Too bad I'm not available," she says. "I'd go out with Brett in a heartbeat."*

*Then she looks at you, puzzled. You know what's coming.*

*"Hey, how come you don't have a boyfriend?" she asks.*

*You dread that question! The fact is, you'd like to have a boyfriend. But you've been told that it's best to wait until you're ready for marriage before you start dating. If only it weren't for . . .*

*"Your religion, right?" the second girl says.*

*'Was she reading my mind?' you think to yourself.*

*"With you it's always Bible, Bible, Bible," she taunts. "Why can't you have a little fun sometimes?"*

HAVE you ever been ridiculed because of trying to live by Bible standards? If so, perhaps you wondered if you were missing out on something. A youth named Deborah felt that way. "Bible standards felt restrictive," she recalls. "My school friends' uninhibited lifestyle appealed to me."

## A Reality Check

Experience is not always the best teacher. In fact, it's both wise and Scriptural to learn from the mistakes of others, as did the psalmist Asaph. For a time, he felt that God's standards were too restrictive. But examining the course of those who had abandoned God's ways gave him a reality check. Asaph later concluded that they were on "slippery ground."—Psalm 73:18.

With that in mind, consider the following comments from youths who, for a time, abandoned Bible standards and became involved in premarital sex.

● **What factors influenced your thinking and actions?**

*Deborah:* "I went through school seeing everyone else having boyfriends and girlfriends, and they seemed to be happy. When I hung out with them and saw them kissing and embracing, I felt jealous and lonely. I often allowed myself to spend hours fantasizing about a certain boy I liked. This heightened my desire to be with him."

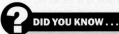

**DID YOU KNOW ...**

It takes only moments to damage your relationship with Jehovah, but it could take years to repair it.

*Mike:* "I read material and watched programs that glorified sex. Talking about sex with my friends heightened my curiosity. Then, when I was alone with a girl, I'd think that I could be physically intimate with her without having sex, that I could stop anytime."

*Andrew:* "I habitually viewed pornography on the Internet. I started drinking a lot of alcohol. And I attended parties with youths who had little respect for the Bible's moral standards."

*Tracy:* "I knew in my mind that premarital sex was wrong, but I didn't hate it. I didn't intend to start a sexual relationship before marriage, but my emotions overrode my thinking. For a while, my conscience was numb to any feelings of guilt."

● **Did your lifestyle make you happy?**

*Deborah:* "At first, I felt a rush of freedom and was happy that I finally fit in with my peers. But those feelings didn't last. I started to feel dirty, robbed of innocence, empty. I felt a deep sense of regret that I'd thrown away my virginity."

*Andrew:* "It became easier and easier to act on wrong desires. But at the same time, I was consumed with feelings of guilt and was disappointed with myself."

*Tracy:* "Immorality ruined my youth. I thought that my boyfriend and I would have such fun. We didn't. We ended up causing each other pain, misery, and heartache. I spent night after night sobbing in bed, wishing I'd done things Jehovah's way."

*Mike:* "I started to feel like part of me had died. I tried to disregard the effect my actions were having on others, but I couldn't. It pained me to realize that in seeking my own pleasure, I was hurting others."

● **What advice would you give to youths who wonder if the Bible's moral standards are too restrictive?**

*Tracy:* "Live by Jehovah's standards, and associate with people who do the same. You will be happier that way."

*Deborah:* "It's not just about you and what you want. Your actions will affect others. And if you ignore God's advice, you will damage yourself."

*Andrew:* "When you're inexperienced, you think your peers' lifestyle is exciting. Their attitudes will rub off on

> **TIP**
>
> **Think of how you would defend the wisdom of Bible standards to a younger sibling. Speaking about your beliefs is a powerful way to solidify them in your heart.**

> **"I, Jehovah, am your God, the One teaching you to benefit yourself."**—Isaiah 48:17.

• • • • • • • •

you. So choose your friends wisely. Trust Jehovah, and you'll save yourself a lot of regrets."

*Mike:* "Among the most valuable possessions Jehovah gives you are your dignity and innocence. To throw those gifts away because you can't control yourself is to sell yourself cheap. Talk to your parents and other mature people about your problems. If you make a mistake, be quick to speak up and correct the situation. If you do things Jehovah's way, you will gain a real sense of peace."

## Bible Standards—Straitjacket or Seat Belt?

Jehovah is "the happy God," and he wants you to be happy too. (1 Timothy 1:11; Ecclesiastes 11:9) The

## >>> action plan!

*To help me understand the wisdom of Bible standards, I will*

...................................................................................................

...................................................................................................

*If I start to envy those who live by the world's standards, I will*

...................................................................................................

...................................................................................................

*What I would like to ask my parent(s) about this subject is*

...................................................................................................

...................................................................................................

# Asaph

Asaph is going through a **difficult time** in his life. All around him he sees people breaking God's laws and seemingly getting away with it! As a result, Asaph wonders if it's worth putting forth the effort to please God. "Surely it is in vain that I have cleansed my heart and that I wash my hands in innocence itself," he says. After giving the matter **deep thought,** though, Asaph changes his mind. He realizes that any enjoyment the wicked experience is only **temporary.** Asaph's conclusion? "Besides you," he tells Jehovah in song, "I do have no other delight on the earth."—Psalm 73:3, 13, 16, 25, 27.

Perhaps at times you have questioned the value of living by God's standards. But be like Asaph, and look **beneath the surface.** Consider the situation of those who have disregarded Jehovah's laws. Are they *really* at peace? Have they found some secret to happiness that those who are faithful to God have missed? After thinking the matter through, you'll no doubt be moved to echo the words of Asaph: "The **drawing near to God** is good for me."—Psalm 73:28.

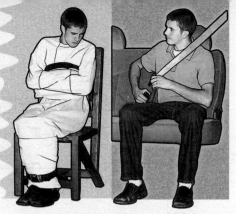

*Bible standards don't restrict your happiness; they protect you*

standards recorded in the Bible are for your benefit. True, you could view them as a straitjacket that limits your freedom. In reality, though, the Bible's moral code is more like a seat belt that helps protect you from harm.

Certainly, you can trust the Bible. If you choose to live by its standards, you'll not only make Jehovah happy but also benefit yourself.—Isaiah 48:17.

**IN OUR NEXT CHAPTER** *You can be God's friend. Find out how.*

## WHAT DO YOU THINK?

- When it comes to the consequences of disobeying God's laws, why is personal experience *not* the best teacher?

- What do you learn from the comments of Deborah, Mike, Andrew, and Tracy?

- Why might some people view Bible standards as a straitjacket, but why is that view shortsighted?

# 35

# How can I become God's friend?

*Through personal tragedy Jeremy came to appreciate the value of having a friendship with God. "When I was 12, my father left our family," he explains. "One night I was praying in bed, begging Jehovah to make my father come back."*

*In his despair, Jeremy began reading his Bible. When he came upon Psalm 10:14, he was profoundly moved. That verse says of Jehovah: "To you the unfortunate one, the fatherless boy, commits himself. You yourself have become his helper." Jeremy says: "I felt that Jehovah was talking to me and letting me know that he was my helper; he was my Father. What better father could I have than him?"*

WHETHER you're in a situation similar to that of Jeremy or not, the Bible indicates that Jehovah *wants* you to be his friend. In fact, the Bible says: "Draw close to God, and he will draw close to you." (James 4:8) Think about what those words mean: Even though you can't see him—and he's certainly not your peer in any sense of the word—Jehovah God is inviting you to be his friend!

But friendship with God will require effort on your part. To illustrate: If you have a houseplant, you know that it doesn't grow on its own. For it to thrive, you have to water it regularly and keep it in an environment that's suitable for growth. The same is true of friendship with God. How can you help such a friendship to grow?

### The Importance of Study

Friendship involves two-way communication—both listening and talking. That's also true of friendship with

*Like a houseplant, friendship with God requires nurturing if it is to grow*

> *When I was younger, my prayers were repetitious. Now I try to pray about the good and the bad points of each particular day. Since no two days are exactly alike, this keeps me from saying the same things over and over.* **—Eve**

God. Reading and studying the Bible is the way we listen to what God has to say to us.—Psalm 1:2, 3.

Granted, study may not be your favorite activity. Many youths would rather watch TV, play a game, or just hang out with friends. But if you want to cultivate friendship with God, there's no shortcut. You'll need to *listen* to him by studying his Word.

Don't worry, though. Bible study doesn't have to be a chore. You can learn to *enjoy* it —even if you don't consider yourself the studying type. The first thing you need to do is *set aside time* for Bible study. "I have a schedule," says a girl named Lais. "I read one chapter of the Bible first thing each morning." Maria, 15, has a different routine. "I read a little of the Bible each night before I go to sleep," she says.

**TIP**

**Read just four pages of the Bible each day, and you'll complete it in about a year.**

To get started on your own study program, look at the box on page 292. Then, below, write down a time when you could spend just 30 minutes or so studying God's Word.

✎ ......................................................................

Scheduling time is just the start. Once you actually begin studying, you might be hit with the reality that the Bible isn't always easy reading. You may agree with 11-year-old

## ⁝⁝ explore your Bible

**1. Select a Bible account that you would like to read.** Pray for wisdom to understand the material.

**2. Read the account carefully.** Take your time. As you read, use your imagination. Engage as many of your senses as you can: Try to see the action, *hear* the voices of the characters, *smell* the air, *taste* the food, and so forth. Make the account come to life in your mind!

**3. Think about what you just read.** Ask yourself questions, such as the following:

● *Why did Jehovah include this account in his Word?*

● *Which characters are worthy of imitation, and which ones serve as warning examples?*

● *What practical lessons can I take away from this reading?*

● *What does the account teach me about Jehovah and the way he does things?*

**4. Say a brief prayer to Jehovah.** Tell him what you learned from your Bible study and how you plan to apply the material in your life. Always thank Jehovah for the gift he has given you—his Word, the Holy Bible!

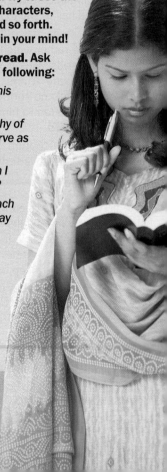

*"Your word is a lamp to my foot, and a light to my roadway."*
—Psalm 119:105.

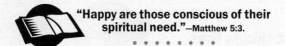

**"Happy are those conscious of their spiritual need."**—Matthew 5:3.

• • • • • • • •

Jezreel, who candidly states, "Some parts of the Bible are heavy going and not very entertaining." If you feel that way, don't give up. Always approach study of the Bible with the view that you're taking time to listen to Jehovah God, your friend. In the end, Bible study will be as exciting and rewarding as you choose to make it!

## Prayer Is Vital

Prayer is the way we talk to God. Think of what an amazing gift prayer is! You can call on Jehovah God at any time of the day or night. He's *always* available. More than that, he *wants* to hear what you have to say. That's why the Bible urges you: "In *everything* by prayer and supplication along with thanksgiving let your petitions be made known to God."—Philippians 4:6.

As that scripture indicates, there are many things you can talk to Jehovah about. These might include your problems and anxieties. They could also include things that you're grateful for. After all, don't you find yourself thanking your friends for the good things they have done for you? You can do the same with Jehovah, who has done more for you than any other friend *ever* could.—Psalm 106:1.

Below, list some things for which *you* are thankful to Jehovah. ✎ ..................................................................

..................................................................

..................................................................

**READ MORE ABOUT THIS TOPIC IN VOLUME 1, CHAPTERS 38 AND 39**

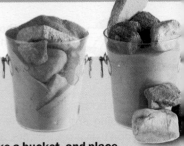

## first things first

*Too busy to pray? No time for Bible study? Often, it comes down to how you set your priorities.*

**Try this experiment:** Take a bucket, and place several large rocks inside it. Now fill the bucket with sand —all the way to the top. You now have a bucket full of rocks *and* sand.

Now empty the bucket, but keep the same sand and rocks. Try the process in reverse: Fill the bucket with sand, and then try to place the rocks inside the bucket. No room? That's because this time you put the sand in the bucket *first.*

The point? The Bible says: "Make sure of the more important things." (Philippians 1:10) If you put small things like recreation in first place, you'll never seem to have enough room in your life for the big things —spiritual pursuits. But if you follow the Bible's admonition, you'll find that you have room for both Kingdom interests *and* a measure of recreation. It's all a matter of what you put in your bucket first!

No doubt there are fears and anxieties that weigh on your mind from time to time. Psalm 55:22 says: "Throw your burden upon Jehovah himself, and he himself will sustain you. Never will he allow the righteous one to totter."

On the following lines, list any personal concerns that you would like to make a matter of prayer.

✎ ......................................................................
......................................................................

**Personal Experience**

There's another aspect of your friendship with God that you shouldn't ignore. The psalmist David wrote: "Taste and see that Jehovah is good." (Psalm 34:8) When David composed the 34th Psalm, he had just been through a frightening experience. He was on the run from murderous King Saul—a harrowing ordeal in itself. But then he had to take refuge among his enemies the Philistines. Faced with what seemed to be certain death, David cleverly disguised his sanity and was able to get away.—1 Samuel 21:10-15.

David didn't attribute his narrow escape to his own ingenuity. Instead, he gave credit to Jehovah. Earlier in the psalm mentioned above, he wrote: "I inquired of Jehovah, and he answered me, and out of all my frights he delivered

## ▷▷▷ action plan!

*To get more out of personal Bible study, I will*

✎ ......................................................................
......................................................................

*To become more regular in my prayers, I will*

......................................................................
......................................................................

*What I would like to ask my parent(s) about this subject is*

......................................................................
......................................................................

me." (Psalm 34:4) It was from *personal experience*, then, that David could urge others to "taste and see that Jehovah is good."*

Can you think of an experience in your life that gives evidence of Jehovah's care? If so, write about it below. Hint: The experience need not be highly dramatic. Try to reflect on simple everyday blessings, some of which may easily be taken for granted.

✎ ............................................................................................

............................................................................................

Perhaps your parents have taught you about the Bible. If so, that's a blessing. Still, you need to develop a *personal* friendship with God. If you haven't done that, you can use the material in this chapter to help you get started. Jehovah will bless your efforts. The Bible says: "Keep on asking, and it will be given you; keep on seeking, and you will find."—Matthew 7:7.

---

* Some Bibles render the phrase "taste and see" as "discover for yourself," "find out for yourself," and "by experience you will see."—*Contemporary English Version, Today's English Version,* and *The Bible in Basic English.*

**IN OUR NEXT CHAPTER** *Find it hard to talk to others about God? Learn how you can defend your beliefs.*

**WHAT DO YOU THINK?**

- ● How can you make personal study of the Bible more enjoyable?

- ● Why does Jehovah want to listen to the prayers of imperfect humans?

- ● How can you improve the quality of your prayers?

36

# How can I defend my belief in God?

***What would most likely hold you back from talking to a classmate about your faith?***

- ☐ Lack of Bible knowledge
- ☐ Fear of ridicule
- ☐ Not knowing how to start a conversation

***Which method of talking about your faith would you find easiest?***

- ☐ Talking one-on-one to a student
- ☐ Speaking before the entire class
- ☐ Writing about my Bible-based beliefs in a report

***Name a schoolmate who you think might be receptive to a Bible discussion if you knew how to bring up the subject.***

......................................

GOD probably isn't the most popular topic of conversation among your schoolmates. Bring up almost anything else—sports, clothes, or the opposite sex—and you'll trigger a lively discussion. But mention God, and an awkward silence may quickly descend.

Not that your peers don't believe in God; many youths *do.* But some are embarrassed to discuss the subject. 'It's just not cool,' they might think.

## What About *You?*

If you're reluctant to talk to your schoolmates about God, it's understandable. No one enjoys being rejected, and being made fun of is even worse! Could that happen if you talked about your faith? It could. On the other hand, your peers might surprise you. Many of them are searching for answers to such questions as: Where is this world heading? and Why is it so full of trouble? Your peers would likely rather talk about those subjects with someone their own age than with an adult.

Still, talking to your peers about *religion* may seem like a daunting challenge. Really, though, you don't have to come across as a fanatic,

*Much like playing a musical instrument, talking about your faith requires skill—with practice, you will become proficient*

> ❝ **School is a preaching territory**
> **that only we can reach.** ❞ —*Iraida*

nor do you have to worry about saying *exactly* the right thing. Talking about your faith can be a little like playing a musical instrument. Challenging at first? Probably. But with practice it becomes easier, and your efforts will pay off. How, though, do you get a conversation started?

Usually, you can find a comfortable opening. For instance, perhaps when a current event is being discussed at school, you can add your Scriptural perspective. Or you could try speaking to just one classmate. Easier still, some Christian youths have simply placed a Bible-based publication on their desk to see if it attracts a classmate's attention. Frequently, it does and a conversation follows!

Which of the above methods could *you* try?

✎ ...............................................................................................

Can you think of another way you could talk about your faith with a classmate? If so, write it below.

.................................................

.................................................

.................................................

Sometimes a school project lends itself to giving a witness about your faith. For example, what might you do when the subject of evolution arises? How can you defend your belief in creation?

| TIP ✔ |
| --- |
| Be aware of your demeanor when you talk about your beliefs. If you appear ashamed, you may *invite* ridicule from your peers. But if you speak with confidence —just as your schoolmates would speak about *their* views— you're more likely to win their respect. |

**"I am not ashamed of the good news; it is, in fact, God's power for salvation to everyone having faith."**—Romans 1:16.

. . . . . . . . .

### Defending Creation

"When evolution was brought up in the classroom, it challenged everything I had been taught," says a youth named Ryan. "It was presented as a fact, and I found that to be intimidating." A girl named Raquel expresses herself similarly. "I was terrified when my social studies teacher said that evolution would be our next lesson," she says. "I knew that I'd have to explain in class where I stood on this controversial issue."

How do *you* feel when the subject of evolution comes up in class? You believe that God "created all things." (Revelation 4:11) You see evidence of intelligent design all around you. But the textbooks say that life evolved, and so does your teacher. Who are you to argue with the "experts"?

Rest assured, you're not alone in your feelings about the evolution theory. The fact is, even a number of scientists don't accept it. Neither do many teachers and students.

Still, to defend your belief in creation, you need to know what the Bible really teaches on the subject. There's no need to make an issue over things that the Bible doesn't directly comment on. Consider a few examples.

You can conquer your fear of defending your beliefs

*My science textbook says that the earth and the solar system have been in existence for billions of years.* The Bible says that the earth and the rest of the universe were in existence before the first creative day. Thus, the earth and the solar system may well be billions of years old.—Genesis 1:1.

*My teacher says that the earth could not have been created in just six days.* The Bible doesn't state that the six creative days were literal 24-hour periods.

*Our class discussed several examples of changes in animals and humans that took place over time.* The Bible says that God created living things "according to their kinds." (Genesis 1:20, 21) It does *not* support the idea that life arose from nonliving matter or that God started off the process of evolution with a single cell. Still, each "kind" has the potential for great variety. So the Bible allows for change to take place *within each "kind."*

In view of what has been considered in this chapter, how would you respond if a teacher or a classmate said:

*"Science has proved that we are the product of evolution."* ✎ ...........................................

..................................................................................................

*"I don't believe in God because I can't see him."*

..................................................................................................

..................................................................................................

## Be Confident of Your Beliefs!

If you're being raised by Christian parents, you might believe in creation simply because that's what you've been taught. Now that you're growing older, though, you want to worship God "with your power of reason," having a solid foundation for your beliefs. (Romans 12:1) In view of that, ask yourself, 'What convinces *me* that there is a Creator?' Sam, 14, looks at the human body. "It's so detailed and complex," he says, "and all of its parts work so well together. The human body couldn't have evolved!" Hol-

## ⟩⟩⟩ action plan!

*To strike up a conversation about the Bible with a classmate, I could*

✎ ...........................................................................................

..................................................................................................

*If I am asked why I believe in a Creator, I will say*

..................................................................................................

..................................................................................................

*What I would like to ask my parent(s) about this subject is*

..................................................................................................

..................................................................................................

ly, 16, agrees. "Since being diagnosed with diabetes," she says, "I have learned a lot about how the body works. It's amazing, for example, how the pancreas—a little organ that hides behind the stomach—does such a huge job in keeping blood and the other organs working."

Below, list three things that convince *you* that there is a Creator.

1. ................................................................................

2. ................................................................................

3. ................................................................................

There's no reason to feel awkward or ashamed because you believe in God and in creation. Considering the evidence, it's entirely reasonable to believe that we humans are the product of intelligent design.

In the end, it's really evolution, not creation, that requires a huge leap of faith—in effect, belief in miracles without a miracle maker! Once you've thought this matter through using your power of reason, you will feel more confident about defending your belief in God.

**IN OUR NEXT CHAPTER** *You see others your age getting baptized. Are you ready to take that step?*

---

**WHAT DO YOU THINK?**

- ● **Why is it important to talk to others about what you believe?**

- ● **What are some ways you can comfortably express your belief in creation at school?**

- ● **How can you show your appreciation for the One who created all things?—Acts 17:26, 27.**

**37**

# Should I get baptized?

*Mark the following statements true or false:*

*Baptism is a requirement for Christians.*
❏ True
❏ False

*The main purpose of baptism is to protect you from giving in to sin.*
❏ True
❏ False

*Baptism puts you in line for salvation.*
❏ True
❏ False

*If you're not baptized, you're not accountable to God for your actions.*
❏ True
❏ False

*If your friends are getting baptized, that means you're ready for baptism too.*
❏ True
❏ False

IF YOU'RE living up to God's standards, cultivating a friendship with God, and talking to others about your faith, it's only natural for you to be thinking about baptism. But how do you know if you're ready for that step? To help answer that question, let's consider the true-or-false statements above.

> **? DID YOU KNOW . . .**
>
> The act of baptism is a vital part of "the mark" that identifies you for salvation.
> —Ezekiel 9:4-6.

**"Present your bodies a sacrifice living, holy, acceptable to God, a sacred service with your power of reason."**—Romans 12:1.

. . . . . . . . .

● *Baptism is a requirement for Christians.*

**True.** Jesus directed that his disciples be baptized. (Matthew 28:19, 20) In fact, Jesus himself submitted to baptism. To follow Christ, you need to be baptized when you're mature enough to make that decision and have a genuine desire to do so.

● *The main purpose of baptism is to protect you from giving in to sin.*

**False.** Baptism is a public symbol of your dedication to Jehovah. Your dedication isn't a cold contract that restrains you from doing things that you would secretly like to do. Rather, you dedicate your life to Jehovah because you *want* to live by his standards.

● *Baptism puts you in line for salvation.*

**True.** The Bible says that baptism is an important step to gaining salvation. (1 Peter 3:21) This doesn't mean, though, that baptism is like an insurance policy that you buy to protect yourself in case disaster should strike. You get baptized because you love Jehovah and want to serve him forever with your whole heart.—Mark 12:29, 30.

> **TIP** ✓
>
> With your parents' help, find someone in the congregation who can assist you to make spiritual progress. —Acts 16:1-3.

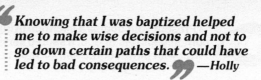

**❝Knowing that I was baptized helped me to make wise decisions and not to go down certain paths that could have led to bad consequences.❞** —Holly

● **If you're not baptized, you're not accountable to God for your actions.**

**False.** James 4:17 states: "If one knows how to do what is right and yet does not do it, it is a sin for him" —baptized or not. So if you know what's right and you're mature enough to take a serious look at your life, perhaps this is the time to talk matters over with a parent or another mature Christian. In that way, you can learn how to progress toward baptism.

● **If your friends are getting baptized, that means you're ready for baptism too.**

**False.** The decision to be baptized needs to come from your own willing heart. (Psalm 110:3) You should be baptized only when you're fully aware of what being one of Jehovah's Witnesses involves and when you're

*(Continued on page 310)*

## ⟫⟫ action plan!

*To progress toward baptism, I will increase my understanding of the following Bible teachings:*

✎ ....................................................................

....................................................................

*What I would like to ask my parent(s) about this subject is*

....................................................................

....................................................................

# ∴ questions often asked about baptism

***What does baptism symbolize?*** Being immersed and raised up means that you have died to a self-seeking course and are now made alive to do Jehovah's will.

***What does it mean to dedicate your life to Jehovah?*** It means to give up ownership of yourself, promising to put the doing of God's will ahead of all else. (Matthew 16:24) It's fitting that you make a formal dedication in prayer to Jehovah sometime before your baptism.

***What should you be doing with your life before baptism?*** You should be living in harmony with God's Word and talking to others about your faith. You should be cultivating a friendship with God through prayer and study of his Word. You should be serving Jehovah because *you* choose to do so—not because others are pressuring you.

***Is there a certain age by which you should be baptized?*** Age is not the primary factor. Still, you should be old enough—and mature enough—to understand the meaning of dedication.

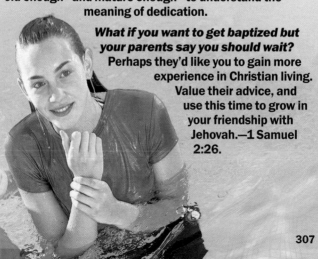

***What if you want to get baptized but your parents say you should wait?*** Perhaps they'd like you to gain more experience in Christian living. Value their advice, and use this time to grow in your friendship with Jehovah.—1 Samuel 2:26.

# ⫶⫶ are you thinking of getting baptized?

Check your progress by considering the questions and statements below. Be sure to look up the cited scriptures before writing your answers.

**In what ways are you currently showing confidence in Jehovah?**—Psalm 71:5.

✎ ...................................................................................

...................................................................................

**How have you demonstrated that your perceptive powers are trained to distinguish right from wrong?**
—Hebrews 5:14.

...................................................................................

...................................................................................

**How often do you pray?**...................................................

**How specific are your prayers, and what do they reveal about your love for Jehovah?**—Psalm 17:6.

...................................................................................

...................................................................................

**List below any goals you would like to set with regard to your prayers.**

...................................................................................

...................................................................................

**How regular is your personal study of the Bible?**
—Joshua 1:8.

...................................................................................

**What do you include in your personal study?**

...................................................................................

...................................................................................

**List below any goals you would like to set with regard to your personal study.**

..............................................................................

**Is your ministry meaningful?** (Examples: Can you explain basic Bible teachings to others? Do you call back on interested ones? Are you working toward conducting a home Bible study?)  ❏ Yes  ❏ No

**Do you engage in the ministry even if your parents do not?** —Acts 5:42.  ❏ Yes  ❏ No

**List below any goals you would like to set with regard to your ministry.** —2 Timothy 2:15.

..............................................................................

..............................................................................

**Would you describe your attendance at Christian meetings as regular or sporadic?** —Hebrews 10:25.

..............................................................................

**In what ways do you participate at meetings?**

..............................................................................

**Do you attend when your parents cannot (if you have their permission to do so)?**  ❏ Yes  ❏ No

**Can you say that you truly delight to do God's will?** —Psalm 40:8.  ❏ Yes  ❏ No

**Can you list specific instances in which you have resisted peer pressure?** —Romans 12:2.

..............................................................................

**How do you plan to keep your love for Jehovah strong?** —Jude 20, 21.

..............................................................................

**Would you serve Jehovah even if your parents and friends stopped doing so?** —Matthew 10:36, 37.  ❏ Yes  ❏ No

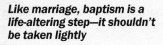

*Like marriage, baptism is a life-altering step—it shouldn't be taken lightly*

*(Continued from page 306)*

sure that you're ready to take on this responsibility.—Ecclesiastes 5:4, 5.

## A Life-Altering Step

Baptism is a life-altering step that leads to many blessings. At the same time, it entails a serious responsibility —that of living up to a personal dedication you've made to Jehovah.

Are you nearing that point? If so, you have good reason to be happy. What lies before you is the greatest privilege of all—that of serving Jehovah wholeheartedly and living in a way that shows that you're truly dedicated to him.—Matthew 22:36, 37.

**IN OUR NEXT CHAPTER** *Learn how to set goals so that you can make the most of your life.*

### WHAT DO YOU THINK?

● Why is baptism such a serious step?

● What might cause a young person to take the step of baptism too soon?

● For what reason might a young person unwisely hold back from dedication and baptism?

# 38

# What will I do with my life?

*"At first, I didn't worry about the future. But as I got closer to graduating from school, I realized that I was going out into the real world, with real jobs. And real bills."—Alex.*

IMAGINE that you're planning a journey that will take you many miles from home. Probably you'd first consult a map to determine the best route. It's similar with planning your future. "You have a wide variety of options," says Michael, a young man who now serves at one of the branch offices of Jehovah's Witnesses. How do you sort through the vast array of choices? "It's all about goals," Michael says.

Think of a goal as a target destination. You're not likely to reach it by wandering about aimlessly. It's far better to pull out a map and plot your course, so to speak. In this way you'll be following the admonition of Proverbs 4:26: "Smooth out the course of your foot." The *Contemporary English Version* renders that phrase: "Know where you are headed."

In the coming years, you'll make many important decisions regarding worship, employment, marriage,

*Having goals will prevent you from expending your energy and getting nowhere*

family, and other vital matters. Wise choices will be easier to make if you first know where you're headed. And as you plot your course in life, there's one factor that you really must not ignore.

## "Remember Your Creator"

To be truly happy, you must take to heart the words of wise King Solomon: "Remember your Creator while you are still young." (Ecclesiastes 12:1, *Today's English Version*) In other words, the choices you make in life should be governed by your desire to please God.

Why is having this priority important? The Bible says at Revelation 4:11: "You are worthy, Jehovah, even our God, to receive the glory and the honor and the power, because you created all things, and because of your will they existed and were created." All creatures in heaven and on earth owe a debt of gratitude to the Creator. Are you

> **I have great admiration for my parents. Their enduring zeal in the ministry, the way they have faced economic hardships, and the encouragement they gave me to share in the full-time ministry, all had a good effect on me.** —Jarrod

thankful that he has given you "life and breath and all things"? (Acts 17:25) Don't you feel compelled to give something back to Jehovah God in appreciation for all that he has given you?

Keeping their Creator close in mind, many youths among Jehovah's Witnesses have pursued the full-time ministry. Consider some of the thrilling avenues of service that may be open to you.

**Pioneering.** Regular pioneers spend an increased amount of time in the ministry. Through training and experience, they sharpen their skills as Bible teachers.

**Serving where there is a greater need.** Some move to an area where there are few Kingdom proclaimers. Others learn a new language and serve with a nearby foreign-language congregation or even move to a foreign land.*

**Missionary service.** Qualified pioneers who have health and stamina are trained for service in foreign lands. Missionaries lead exciting, fulfilling lives.

| TIP | ✔ |
| --- | --- |

**Talk to some who have been in the full-time ministry for many years. Find out why they chose such a career and how they feel they have been blessed.**

_____
* See the box on page 164.

## ⠶ my goals

Check off which goals you would like to set. Use the spaces provided to customize those goals or to create new ones.

### Ministry Goals
✎ ❏ Increase my time in the ministry to ....... hours per month
❏ Place ............ pieces of literature each month
❏ Use the Bible when talking about my faith
❏ Make ............ return visits each month
❏ Start a Bible study

Other goals: ..........................................................................

..........................................................................................

### Study Goals
❏ Read ............ pages of the Bible each day
❏ Prepare for the weekly meetings
❏ Research the following Bible topics:

..........................................................................................

..........................................................................................

### Congregation Goals
❏ Offer at least one comment during each meeting
❏ Strike up a conversation with an older person I'd like to get to know better
❏ Visit an elderly or infirm member of the congregation

Other goals: ..........................................................................

Today's Date ...............................
*Check back in six months, and see how you've done in reaching your goals. Adjust them or add to them as needed.*

> " 'Test me out . . . ,' Jehovah of armies has said, 'whether I shall not open to you people the floodgates of the heavens and actually empty out upon you a blessing until there is no more want.' "—Malachi 3:10.

• • • • • • •

**Bethel service.** Bethel family members serve in branch offices of Jehovah's Witnesses. In some lands this involves the production and shipping of Bible literature.

**International service.** International servants travel to other lands to aid in the construction of Kingdom Halls, Assembly Halls, and branch facilities.

**Ministerial Training School.** Qualified unmarried elders and ministerial servants are trained in organizational matters and in public speaking. Some graduates take on a foreign assignment.

## Plotting Your Course

The full-time ministry is a noble goal, and it brings countless blessings. Forethought, though, will be needed. For example, ask yourself, 'What abilities and skills do I have that I could use to support myself?'

Kelly had a clear goal of becoming a pioneer, so she plotted her course when it came to employment. "I had to choose something that would allow me to support myself in my ministry," she says.

*For more information, watch the DVD "Young People Ask—What Will I Do With My Life?" It is available in more than 30 languages*

Kelly enrolled in a vocational program in high school. This helped her to achieve her primary goal. "The full-time ministry was what I wanted to do," Kelly says. "Everything else was secondary." Kelly is happy with her choice. "I feel my decision was the best one that I could have made," she says.

### Ask for Directions

If you were traveling in an unfamiliar area, at some point you would likely need to ask for directions. You can do the same when planning your future. Get the input of others. Proverbs 20:18 says: "By counsel plans themselves are firmly established."

Your parents are one vital resource. But you can also seek the advice of other mature Christians whose life re-

## ▶ action plan!

*To help me get more joy in the ministry, I will talk to*

✎ ..............................................................................

*What I would like to ask my parent(s) about this subject is*

..............................................................................

..............................................................................

flects godly wisdom. "Look at those who are good examples as adults in your congregation or nearby areas," recommends Roberto, a Bethel family member in his 20's.

More than anyone else, Jehovah God wants to help you make choices in life that will give you the greatest happiness. So ask him to help you 'go on perceiving what his will is' regarding your future. (Ephesians 5:17) In every aspect of your life, follow the admonition of Proverbs 3:5, 6: "Trust in Jehovah with all your heart and do not lean upon your own understanding. In all your ways take notice of him, and he himself will make your paths straight."

## WHAT DO YOU THINK?

- **What abilities and skills do you have?**

- **In what ways can you use your abilities to praise Jehovah?**

- **Which particular form of full-time service mentioned in this chapter appeals to you most?**

*my journal*

*What obstacles might hinder you from reaching your spiritual goals?*

✎ _____

_____

_____

_____

_____

_____

_____

*What specific steps can you take to deal with those obstacles?*

_____

_____

_____

_____

_____

_____

_____

# worksheet
## locator

*More information online!*
*Log on to www.watchtower.org/ype*

# Would you welcome more information?

Write to Jehovah's Witnesses at the appropriate address below.

**ALBANIA:** Kutia postare 118, Tiranë. **ANGOLA:** Caixa Postal 6877, Luanda Sul. **ANTIGUA:** Box 119, St. John's. **ARGENTINA:** Casilla de Correo 83 (Suc 27B), C1427WAB Ciudad Auton. de Bs. As. **AUSTRALIA:** Box 280, Ingleburn, NSW 1890. **AUSTRIA:** Postfach 67, A-1134 Vienna. **BAHAMAS:** Box N-1247, Nassau, NP. **BARBADOS, W.I.:** Crusher Site Road, Prospect, BB 24012 St. James. **BELGIUM:** rue d'Argile-Potaardestraat 60, B-1950 Kraainem. **BENIN:** 06 B.P. 1131, Akpakpa pk3, Cotonou. **BOLIVIA:** Casilla 6397, Santa Cruz. **BRAZIL:** Caixa Postal 92, 18270-970 Tatuí-SP. **BRITAIN:** The Ridgeway, London NW7 1RN. **CAMEROON:** BP 889, Douala. **CANADA:** P.O. Box 4100, Georgetown, ON L7G 4Y4. **CENTRAL AFRICAN REPUBLIC:** BP 662, Bangui. **CHILE:** Casilla 267, Puente Alto. **COLOMBIA:** Apartado Postal 85058, Bogotá. **CONGO, DEMOCRATIC REPUBLIC OF:** B. P. 634, Limete, Kinshasa. **COSTA RICA:** Apartado 187-3006, 40104 Barreal de Heredia. **CÔTE D'IVOIRE:** 06 BP 393, 06 Abidjan. **CROATIA:** p.p. 58, HR-10090 Zagreb-Susedgrad. **CURAÇAO, NETHERLANDS ANTILLES:** PO Box 4708, Willemstad. **CYPRUS:** P O Box 11033, CY-2550 Dali. **CZECH REPUBLIC:** PO Box 90, 198 21 Prague 9. **DENMARK:** P B 340, DK-4300 Holbæk. **DOMINICAN REPUBLIC:** Apartado 1742, Santo Domingo. **ECUADOR:** Casilla 09-01-1334, Guayaquil. **EL SALVADOR, C.A.:** Apartado Postal 401, San Salvador. **ESTONIA:** Postbox 1075, 10302 Tallinn. **ETHIOPIA:** PO Box 5522, Addis Abeba. **FIJI:** Box 23, Suva. **FINLAND:** Postbox 68, FI-01301 Vantaa. **FRANCE:** BP 625, F-27406 Louviers cedex. **FRENCH GUIANA:** 328 CD 2, Route du Tigre, 97300 Cayenne. **GERMANY:** Am Steinfels, 65618 Selters. **GHANA:** PO Box GP 760, Accra. **GREECE:** 77 Kifisias Ave., Marousi, GR 151 24 Athens. **GUADELOUPE, F.W.I.:** Montmain, 97180 Sainte Anne. **GUAM:** 143 Jehovah St, Barrigada, GU 96913. **GUATEMALA:** Apartado postal 711, 01901-Guatemala. **GUYANA:** 352-360 Tyrell St, Republic Park Phase 2 EBD. **HAITI:** PO Box 185, Port-au-Prince. **HAWAII:** 2055 Kamehameha IV Road, Honolulu, HI 96819. **HONDURAS:** Apartado 147, Tegucigalpa. **HONG KONG:** 4 Kent Road, Kowloon Tong, Kowloon. **HUNGARY:** Budapest, Pf. 20, H-1631. **ICELAND:** Sogavegur 71, IS-108 Reykjavík. **INDIA:** Post Box No. 6441, Yelahanka, Bangalore-KAR 560 064. **INDONESIA:** P.O. Box 2105, Jakarta 10001. **IRELAND:** Newcastle, Greystones, Co. Wicklow. **ISRAEL:** PO Box 29345, 61293 Tel Aviv. **ITALY:** Via della Bufalotta 1281, I-00138 Rome RM. **JAMAICA:** PO Box 103, Old Harbour. **JAPAN:** 4-7-1 Nakashinden, Ebina City, Kanagawa-Pref, 243-0496. **KENYA:** Box 21290, 00505 Nairobi. **KOREA, REPUBLIC OF:** Box 33, Pyungtaek P. O., Kyunggi-do 450-600. **KYRGYZSTAN:** Post Box 80, 720080 Bishkek. **LIBERIA:** PO Box 10-0380, 1000 Monrovia 10. **LUXEMBOURG:** B. P. 2186, L-1021 Luxembourg. **MADAGASCAR:** BP 116, 105 Ivato. **MALAWI:** Box 30749, Lilongwe 3. **MALAYSIA:** Peti Surat No. 580, 75760 Melaka. **MARTINIQUE:** B.P. 585, 97207 Fort de France Cedex. **MAURITIUS:** Rue Baissac, Petit Verger, Pointe aux Sables. **MEXICO:** Apartado Postal 896, 06002 Mexico, DF. **MOZAMBIQUE:** Caixa Postal 2600, Maputo. **MYANMAR:** PO Box 62, Yangon. **NETHERLANDS:** Noordbargerstraat 77, NL-7812 AA Emmen. **NEW CALEDONIA:** B P 1741, 98874 Pont des Francais. **NEW ZEALAND:** PO Box 75142, Manurewa, Manukau 2243. **NICARAGUA:** Apartado 3587, Managua. **NIGERIA:** P.M.B. 1090, Benin City 300001, Edo State. **NORWAY:** Gaupeveien 24, NO-1914 Ytre Enebakk. **PANAMA:** Apdo. 0819 - 07567, Panama. **PAPUA NEW GUINEA:** PO Box 636, Boroko, NCD 111. **PARAGUAY:** Casilla de Correo 482, 1209 Asunción. **PERU:** Apartado 18-1055, Lima 18. **PHILIPPINES:** PO Box 2044, 1060 Manila. **POLAND:** ul. Warszawska 14, PL-05830 Nadarzyn. **PORTUGAL:** Apartado 91, P-2766-955 Estoril. **PUERTO RICO:** PO Box 3980, Guaynabo, PR 00970. **ROMANIA:** Căsuţa Poştală nr. 132, OP 39, Bucureşti. **RUSSIA:** PO Box 182, 190000 St. Petersburg. **RWANDA:** BP 529, Kigali. **SLOVAKIA:** PO Box 2, 830 04 Bratislava 34. **SLOVENIA:** p.p. 22, SI-1241 Kamnik. **SOLOMON ISLANDS:** PO Box 166, Honiara. **SOUTH AFRICA:** Private Bag X2067, Krugersdorp, 1740. **SPAIN:** Apartado 132, 28850 Torrejón de Ardoz (Madrid). **SRI LANKA:** 711 Station Road, Wattala 11300. **SURINAME:** PO Box 2914, Paramaribo. **SWEDEN:** Box 5, SE-732 21 Arboga. **SWITZERLAND:** P O Box 225, 3602 Thun. **TAHITI, FRENCH POLYNESIA:** B.P. 7715, 98719 Taravao. **TAIWAN:** 3-12 Shetze Village, Hsinwu 32746. **TANZANIA:** Box 7992, Dar es Salaam. **THAILAND:** P.O. Box 7 Klongchan, Bangkok 10 240. **TOGO:** B.P. 2983, Lomé. **TRINIDAD AND TOBAGO:** Lower Rapsey Street & Laxmi Lane, Curepe. **UKRAINE:** PO Box 955, 79491 Lviv - Briukhovychi. **UNITED STATES OF AMERICA:** 25 Columbia Heights, Brooklyn, NY 11201-2483. **URUGUAY:** Casilla 17030, César Mayo Gutiérrez 2645 y Cno. Varzi, 12500 Montevideo. **VENEZUELA:** Apartado 20.364, Caracas, DC 1020A. **ZAMBIA:** P.O. Box 33459, 10101 Lusaka. **ZIMBABWE:** Private Bag WG-5001, Westgate. **www.watchtower.org**